Between HEAVEN and Ground ZERO

LESLIE HASKIN

Between
HEAVEN
and
Ground
ZERO

BETHANYHOUSE
MINNEAPOLIS, MINNESOTA

Published by Bethany House Publishers
11400 Hampshire Avenue South
Bloomington, Minnesota 55438

Bethany House Publishers is a division of
Baker Publishing Group, Grand Rapids, Michigan.

Printed in the United States of America

ISBN-13:   978-0-7642-0286-5

TO FIREFIGHTERS
AND POLICE OFFICERS
EVERYWHERE . . .

Acknowledgments

First is God my Father!

I believe the Lord fills our lives with wonderful things and unbelievable people when we need them most. I believe in angels. And what I needed most in my recovery besides His arms was the freedom to cry and angels I could trust with my tears.

"Thank you Lord, for sharing your angels with me."

Thank you for Monai Holloway, Avor Alexander, Hank and Helga Schieble, Dr. William Rohan, and Sean Young. Thank you so much for those who helped to save my life: Ronald Smith, Eliot Hill, Dr. Ariella Morris, Marcia Kissel, Pastor John Torres, and my big brother and bestest friend, Pastor Lawrence Haskin.

This book is testimony that the arms of God are far reaching, but it would not have happened had it not been for the sensitivity and vision of two men: Greg Johnson and Jeff Braun.

Truly, I thank God for all of the angels in my life!

Selah

Contents

A Note to the Reader

The story of September 11, 2001, is very complex. It involves seven massive buildings, thousands of people, psychological, emotional, and physical distress, and possibly twenty thousand personal accounts of that day.

This is just one of them.

I suffer from post-traumatic stress disorder.

Post-traumatic stress disorder, or PTSD, is a psychiatric disorder that can come about after one has experienced or witnessed life-threatening events like war, natural disasters, terrorist incidents, or violent personal assaults.

There are many symptoms to this disorder. Most of mine involved the psycho-physiological changes associated with PTSD like hyper-arousal of the sympathetic nervous system, flashbacks, increased sensitivity of the startle reflex, memory loss, and sleep abnormalities. There were others, but these affected me most.

Exposure therapy and drug treatments are most common. My treatments involved medication and a very aggressive treatment called eye movement desensitization and reprocessing (EMDR), which involves having the patient repeatedly relive the experience under controlled conditions to help work through the trauma.

I assure you that it is extremely difficult to take.

Along with treatment, and to help me first remember and then process what I remembered, I began keeping a journal. These pages represent what I recorded in my journal. By no means is it intended to represent the complete story or historical data. There are still many facts missing—pieces that I might never have to connect the dots—but this is what I remember and what I feel. I hope it brings something valuable to your life.

Continue in God's grace. . . .

Leslie

Introduction

It begins.

On the clear and sunny morning of Tuesday, September 11, 2001, terrorists murdered more than twenty-seven hundred people in an attack on New York City.

Thousands died when at the height of the morning rush, an American Airlines–piloted missile slammed into Tower One of the World Trade Center.

It was first blood.

President Bush vowed that terrorism "will not stand," "God Bless America" was quickly reinstated as our song, American flags decorated our porches, and thousands of American households finally fell asleep each night to the white noise of TV Land and *I Love Lucy.*

Life changed for all of America in a matter of a few grave moments between a deviant cockpit and the ninety-fifth floor.

I have lived and relived those moments at least a million times. A million times lost and searching for words to describe what happened on the inside—the torment and vulnerability, the confusion, the carnage, and the sheer visceral terror of it all. I struggle still in my description of witnessing the heart of humanity colliding with gravity and of dreams of the slaughtered Twin Towers covered in dust and blood while a somber last breath cries for justice.

Nothing in my life prepared me for what I lived through, and I will never forget . . . those stairs . . . the smells . . . those sounds . . . the faces of the people.

My soul yet sings its solemn song, and the severity of that day pours through these pages like a stream . . . so brace yourself.

Every one of us who lived that day has a story to tell about that day, where the terror began and when the nightmare ended.

This is my story, not intended to be a political statement or a means to achieve any bit of self-promotion, false enlightenment, or self-interest. My objective here is to be a gentle light to a world I view as searching.

My hope in this is to speak to all those left with questions and those still mourning—that your faith might be restored. My prayer is that through your grief, anger, consternation, confusion, or resolve, the Lord opens the eyes of your heart so that you will see the hope of His calling. For it is in the midst of uncertainty that the sound of His voice and the silence that follows quiets your inhibitions, and you receive comfort and then clarity, deliverance, and then closure.

Amen.

PART ONE

In the Beginning

CHAPTER I

Eight Million Stories

One Song

It doesn't matter what brings us to that
place, only that we get there and what we
leave owning.

—AUTHOR UNKNOWN

February 20, 2005
1:30 P.M.

It was cold outside. The earth gave off gray nuances and the sun's rays teased the sky. I love the way it looks when God's breath meets with mine in the open air—something so big joining with something so small to create a vapor so eternal. It reminds me that life is the only idea of something I can touch. It moves me beyond words—at least now it does.

I got off the PATH train at the place where it all began. The hair stood up on the back of my neck. Nothing happened in particular . . . not really. Except that when my brain registered the location of my body and my foot hit the platform, forty-two months of spirits and fear, and anger, and hope and pain and surrender, and guilt, and confusion and resolve, and confrontation and nightmares, and every prayer that ever was prayed for me collided in my world. They landed square on my shoulders, collapsed me at the knees, and delivered me to 8:46 A.M. on Tuesday, September 11, 2001. I smelled it all . . . all over again, and I wanted to puke.

> I watched the mounds of dirt breathe, half expecting them to give birth to two towers.

I looked around. It was all so familiar and yet nothing was as I remembered. I could place every building and every person exactly as they last were. For four hours I walked around that enormous, conflicting tomb, begging the cosmos to infuse me with some answers that made even a tiny bit of sense. I watched the mounds of dirt breathe, half expecting them to give birth to two towers . . . as if Rome was built in a day.

Crowds of people gathered around that empty lot. Correction, hundreds gawked at an empty tomb. Wait a minute, at a place like this there are no "mere" people. There are artists creating, writing rhymes, making music and song. There are no individuals, just stories. They say eight million of them compose this naked city. Mine is now a song that bellows and respires in the air, is unintelligible in dreams, and somehow gains vibrato in the open catacombs of Tower One of the World Trade Center.

For this is where I died . . .
This is where I was I born.
This song is the one that I was created to sing.
. . . it took me forever to get
                                    here.

CHAPTER 2

September 11

Perfect in Beauty

The Mighty One, God, the Lord, speaks and summons the earth from the rising of the sun to the place where it sets. From Zion, perfect in beauty, God shines forth.

—PSALM 50:1–2

September 11, 2001
5:15 A.M.

It was more than a beautiful morning. The sun was already beginning to show her face over the mountains near my home and the sky was a brilliant blue. The kind of blue you see in island waters that once glanced, imprints itself a lasting image. Birds were singing and the wind was calm and gentle with the scent of fresh flowers and cleanly cut grass. The air was stimulating. Everything was alive! It was the kind of day that inspired being in love and the appreciation of love. It was a day that brought beauty to perfection.

I wanted to skip going to the office that day. I wanted to play hooky and relax in my garden or take a long drive through the mountains to enjoy God's wonder. But duty called.

My days often began early and ended late. It only bothered me on days like these. I would have much preferred sneakers, jeans, and a T-shirt to the Barami suit and one-inch designer pumps I was wearing. It would have pleased me immensely to pack a picnic basket. Instead, I was stuffing my laptop into its ugly black bag and readying myself for the office. The hour was getting late so I got dressed and reluctantly drove to the train station.

6:20 A.M.
Train I

The station was only seventeen minutes from my home. The views of the mountains between here and there are spectacular. The trees are like picture-perfect heads of broccoli seated at the foot of heaven. The blue sky provides a magnificent canvas.

> Commuting was like work in itself and nothing to look forward to.

Usually I enjoyed the drive—sixty-five miles per hour in a forty-five-mile-per-hour zone along a country road. Usually it was invigorating. Usually jazz radio provided the ambience for my early-morning escape. This morning, however, there were better things to do than take that particular drive and go into the city. Hence, it was a punishment and it seemed to take forever.

Commuting was like work in itself and nothing to look forward to; at best, it could be taxing. I lived about two hours from my office and had to take two trains to get there. Both trains demanded skill and good timing to ride successfully, and after eight years of practice, my timing was still not the best. I pulled into the station just as the train arrived.

Every morning it screeched into my station almost empty. By the second stop, it filled with a cast of colorful characters.

Jack, the conductor, knew all of the everyday riders by name. He was a friendly thirty-five-year-plus railroad veteran whom most thought to be a workaholic. He worked two jobs, ran his own limousine company, never took a sick day, and worked half of his vacation time. Kudos to Jack, because at nearly seventy, his energy was inspiring.

The ride into the city was always uneventful; there was never anything new. We had only to look forward to the same worn leather seats, the same smell of newspaper, and the same cliques of riders. The more popular ones sat in the middle of the train car every day so as not to miss anything. They were the ones in the know. They were the ones who started and ran the rumor mill, laughed the loudest, and tried desperately to create a commuter vibe. They were the ones who, between my naps, kept me amused.

I remember three of them very well. Jan was a young, impressionable legal assistant who likely believed that the louder she talked the more probable it was that she was right. She was a tall, slender woman with dark hair. Most of the men smiled when she sat near them.

Lorna was another commuter. A financial advisor and my favorite to watch, this beautiful plus-sized woman wore her makeup and hair flawlessly styled. Judging from all the advice she gave, she was gold at heart. Her laugh was contagious.

Finally, there was Paul. He stood about five-foot-seven, one hundred fifty pounds—a reasonably attractive "professional commuter." No one really knew exactly what he did for a living, but every morning he boarded the train and announced his arrival by greeting every woman within earshot with a smile and a copy of his pay stub—not really, but when all else fails . . .

There were others, of course, but none quite as entertaining or that I enjoyed more. These few invested a lot in surviving the everyday madness of commuter travel. I respected their determination to take it all in stride.

I like to think that somehow I remained outside the "center stage" of the commuter regulars—safely set apart and just watching. On occasion, though, I might have been in the middle of it all.

I am a peculiar sort. Unlike many others, my personality does not match my chosen career. They are, in fact, literal opposites that nonetheless complement the two very strong aspects of my "self."

On the one hand, I am a thinker and quite cerebral. I am an evaluator with a very low tolerance for anything destructive, especially people. I am candid, introspective, and quite often misunderstood. In other words, I can be opinionated. On the other hand, I am an easygoing, lively risk-taker who loves life and appreciates most things that give me a challenge. I love laughter and walking in the mountains. I am strong, grounded, and I fear nothing . . . well, maybe birds. I have struggled with asthma since childhood but at every opportunity will defy even that. I am a fighter. I stand about five feet tall with a somewhat athletic build. I have big eyes, a broad face, and when I am awake, I am usually smiling.

I enjoy quiet time. So for me, commuting time, unlike the core group, was nap time. I always sat alone and spread out over the large

Amtrak-ish seats, rested my head on the very cold, hard window, and snored.

This was my routine, my crew, and my mornings. It was my life every Monday through Friday of every week in every month of every year. I was a commuter, like it or not.

7:58 A.M.
Train 2

When I arrived at the Hoboken train terminal, people were already racing for the next PATH train. The "PATH," the second and final train in my long haul into the city, connects New Jersey transit lines to the New York City subway system. It went directly into the subfloors of the World

> It is glamorous and degenerate, cultured and crude, beautiful and detestable, ethical and decadent, exciting and scary all at the same time.

Trade Center. Our office was on the thirty-fifth and thirty-sixth floors of the north tower, known as Tower One.

Anxious commuters check their watches every two minutes and pack the platform in wait. As bizarre as it is, they stand close to the platform's edge and lean in to be the first to spot a train that screams when it arrives. They rush forward at first sight, then back away from the tracks as the train pulls in.

New York trains are infamous for "pushers." Most people push to get on and get a seat, and then push their way off to be first on the escalators. I always felt it best to stand near a door and let the surge take me both ways.

Riding this rail is an adventure, to put it mildly. It is always crowded, late, and smelly. The floors are sometimes sticky and littered with "God only knows what." It is best compared to New York City itself . . . in motion . . . somewhat difficult to describe. It is the perfect contradiction: It is glamorous and degenerate, cultured and crude, beautiful and detestable, ethical and decadent, exciting and scary all at the same time.

The PATH, like downtown Manhattan Island, is a stage for the homeless. They find their audience here and perform through their hunger. In watching, I am both confused and bothered by their signs. And the Negro spirituals that flow from the mouths of these dirty-blond men embarrass me.

That morning the train filled as always. I squeezed on just before the door closed. The person on my right gave me a dirty look as the not so very gentle man on my left gave me a shove. I assumed their disapproval but ignored them both. It was a short ride, not worth the fight, just fifteen minutes tops to the World Trade Center, the train's last stop and our liberation.

CHAPTER 3

Tower One

The "It," the Ego . . .

Their land is full of silver and gold; there is
no end to their treasures. Their land is full
of horses; there is no end to their chariots.
Their land is full of idols; they bow down to
the work of their hands, to what their
fingers have made.

—ISAIAH 2:7–8

8:10 A.M.
All Towers

I loved working at the World Trade Center, with its regal towers. I loved the convenience and status of it all: the shops, restaurants, and tourists who came from all over the world to see its unique majesty. I basked in the pampering of daily concerts on the plaza and activities around the huge fountains. I never tired of it.

Architecturally, the World Trade Center was the union of seven buildings connected by an above-street plaza and a concourse. The most famous of these buildings were the Twin Towers, or the "Twins." These were incredible and massive giants. They stood more than thirteen hundred feet high, with 110 floors. About nine million square feet of office space housed more than fifty thousand workers and served more than seventy thousand visitors on any given day. The main lobby of the towers boasted tons of beautiful windows spanning more than one hundred feet from floor to ceiling.

Its marble floors and walls were astounding, rising toward extravagant chandeliers that caught rays of natural light and generously distributed it into otherwise obscure or unworthy lobby corners. This was a grand building, tasteful, exquisite, and beaming from the light of the sun.

Outside each entrance were beautiful stone flower planters, almost as grand as the building itself. Designers created every planter, using polished stone and seasonal flowers, the scent of which, when riding a subtle breeze, was in itself masterful.

> This was an unforgettable place. Unmistakably built to captivate and maintained to seduce.

The concourse was home to several delis, restaurants, and all the finer shops like Louis Vuitton, Tourneau, Barami, and others. Once inside you could walk for miles, shop, eat, and socialize without ever going outside. The strong walls of the concourse were massive and decorated with fine art, advertisements, and everything that was New York—sweeter than an apple and bigger than big city blues.

If you have never been to the Trade Center, then you've been cheated. If you have, then you're most likely still there. This was an unforgettable place. Unmistakably built to captivate and maintained to seduce.

Walking through the World Trade Center during the morning rush was much the same as walking through the World Trade Center at night or midday. It was always busy with people.

The Twins housed nearly three hundred businesses. They were home to law firms, insurance houses, brokerage firms, government agencies, entertainment management companies, and other businesses wanting that prestigious address. Most offices began their day at about 7:30 with dedicated employees at their desks and working. It was almost a privilege. This was a warm, welcoming house of natural stones, metal, and glass, and it was busy . . . always.

By 8:00, there were already thousands of workers, shoppers, and adoring fans rushing who knows where. The sound of hustling feet resonated through the concourse and outlasted the sound of their unintelligible conversations.

That morning was no exception. There were early-bird tourists taking pictures and excited hotel guests looking for maps and asking questions. Most stores were open and people were already browsing. Breakfast meetings were underway and the aroma of deli food mingled with the smell of detergent as maintenance personnel busied themselves with their work.

From every corner of the concourse, one could see vendors just outside doors, intruding on time with their cloth-covered tables bearing an assortment of what they called "goods" for sale. They sold everything imaginable—fruit, clothes, jewelry, shoes, and even electronics.

Celebrities, politicians, and international tourists frequented this place. It was one of New York's finest. It was awe-inspiring, and like the day, it was a masterpiece, beautiful and alive.

8:23 A.M.

I stepped quickly through the crowd and to my favorite deli. It was located on the lower level of the Trade Center near the PATH's exit, so there was always a line. Sam, the owner, was waiting for me with my usual cranberry muffin and hazelnut coffee. I made my purchase and then made my way up the escalators and to the elevators.

I often played a little game with myself as I approached the lobby doors. I would count my footsteps in contrast to the person walking next to me. I liked the rhythm it produced—nothing important really, just something my friends would call a Leslie-*ism*.

That morning, security staffed their stations as they always did, precisely and expertly. They stood with their intentional smiles, directing visitors here and there and asking to see access badges— nothing extraordinary.

I walked with my usual arrogant and confident strut, swinging my laptop bag and firmly gripping my coffee. My mind wandered a bit in anticipation of hazelnut flavoring and cranberries. As I approached the lobby, I swiped my security pass and jumped onto the already crowded elevator. I did this much like I boarded the train, just before the door closed. I got the same looks of disapproval and ignored them just the same. I felt lucky that morning because some kind someone didn't let the door close in my face. To me, that was a sign it was going to be a great day.

CHAPTER 4

. . . and the Super Ego

Above It All

My company's office space was a beautiful example of an over-inflated facilities budget. The reception area, located directly in front of the elevator bank, was separated by etched glass doors and decorated with large floor plants and fresh flowers delivered weekly. Natural wood-grained furniture was consistent throughout the more than forty thousand square feet on each floor. Equal in extravagance were the bathroom tiles flown in from Italy.

Like every other floor in the tower, we had floor-to-ceiling windows about two feet wide, separated by narrower columns. Even from ten feet away, one could look out and into the skies or look down on the city and feel above it all. That's how working in the towers felt . . . above it all.

Cubicles, or "cubes," varying in size and location, engaged most of our office space. They were symmetrical, but cleverly positioned so as not to intrude on management's tasteful and luxurious corner office views. Underwriting assistants occupied most of the cubes. There was no rhyme or reason to assigning them, except maybe the more overambitious the manager, the larger the assistant's space. The cubes just outside of the executive offices were most coveted. They had breathtaking views of the city and were a sign of success and power.

My assistant's cube was directly in front of the northeast-facing window.

I had a big title, a bigger salary, and a huge ego.

One of only two African-American directors in the northeast region, I headed the operations department for one of the largest insurance companies in the country. My division was comprised of facilities, management information systems, branch services, about one-third of the underwriting staff, and their underwriting assistants. I had a big title, a bigger salary, and a huge ego.

I like to think that I managed my staff with fairness and that they liked me. The truth is, my arrogance probably overshadowed my sense of fair play in most situations and my staff hated to see me coming.

> See that you are not troubled; for all these things must come to pass, but the end is not yet. For nation will rise against nation and kingdom against kingdom. And there will be famines, pestilences, and earthquakes in various places. All these things are the beginning of sorrows. (Matthew 24:6–8 NKJV)

And so . . . my day begins.

8:28 A.M.

I got off the elevator on the thirty-sixth floor and walked the few hundred feet from reception through common office space and to my private office. I did that morning as I always did, with a swift purposeful strut. I paused only for the usual forced smiles, nods, and good mornings. I took mental note of those working and those pretending to work in order that I might later make someone's day with a big project that afforded them no time for pretense.

No sooner had I powered up my computer and begun checking my e-mails, when my phone rang. This was typical of my mornings. I ignored it. Everyone knew I wasn't alive until after my first full cup of coffee. I sat, delighted by the smell, and quietly sipped in the morning.

Approximately 8:43 A.M.

A few sips of coffee later, I decided to go over to my very envied assistant's desk for some quick answers. I knew from the night before that a problem with one of our major policyholders needed resolution. The idea was to appease my need to be in control and to get an explanation simple enough so as not to complicate my breakfast.

I liked keeping these types of exchanges short and to the point. We traded pleasantries and got to the problem at hand. In mid-sentence, suddenly and without warning, the building shook violently and thunder came from within. It swayed back and forth slowly for a few seconds, as if riding a calm wave, and then stopped. It paralyzed any fair semblance of time.

From that precise second, time was both accelerated and suspended.

CHAPTER 5

Strike One

Pass Me Not, O Gentle Savior

Disaster will come upon you, and you will

not know how to conjure it away.

A calamity will fall upon you that you

cannot ward off with a ransom;

a catastrophe you cannot foresee will

suddenly come upon you.

—ISAIAH 47:11

I WAS EIGHTEEN YEARS OLD when cancer claimed my mother's life. *It was a fight to the finish and she was a most worthy opponent.*

Momma, or "Madea" as she was lovingly called, was short in stature but a giant in personality. She had a beautiful light tan complexion and the deepest eyes I had ever seen as a child. Still now, there are no comparisons. It sounds cliché, but her smile could awaken the stars at noon. Her effortless and natural love for life and people radiated through her presence. It could overwhelm at times—at least it did me.

She was playful and enjoyed the practical jokes she pulled on each of her children. Equal to her playful nature was the fight in her. She was strong and steadfast in her convictions with a faith in God that was without question or condition. Her faith was her legacy.

It was Momma's huge voice and love for music that directed our church choir. Her voice was as big and as beautiful as she was—and when she sang, Momma sang! Her soulful, raspy voice grabbed you in the gut and made you know "There is a God." Sometimes her voice floated around in my head for hours, singing: "Pass me not, O gentle Savior . . . Hear my humble cry . . . While on others Thou art calling . . . Do not pass me by."

Sometimes on Saturday mornings she would sit in front of her piano, playing without restraint and singing. Her hands glided effortlessly, tickling the ivories, with her eyes closed and head tossed back. She would sing until the neighbors woke up. We call it praise and worship today. Back then, it was simply disturbing the peace. "Leslie," she'd say, "praise God always, in good and bad times, because we know that all things work together for good to them that love Him."

I hated hearing that. I hated that she forced me to learn to play the piano, and I hated having a mother stronger than a riptide direct from the ocean floor in mid-August. I defied her at *every turn, but she forced her wisdom on me. She forced me to listen, and somehow I learned.*

I learned from her songs, her family meetings, and her unique ability to feed her children the cold, hard truth and somehow make it okay. Her arms were our safe place. We knew that when we were there, nothing could harm us, not even life.

I would love nothing better than to honestly say that I went quickly to my safe place in that moment, or that I sensed my mother's presence with me, but I didn't. I had no senses at all except for those in my feet, which by now were exacting downward as the once stable floor beneath them was in full tilt.

The sound and feel of the impact were indivisible. It was huge. The thunder replaced the beat of my heart. The building rocked from side to side. People swore as they lost their footing and stumbled. Most were already in tears. I was shaking and disoriented.

Loud bangs resonated from the north side of the office. Each time they were so sudden and so random that I nearly jumped out of my skin. There was a nonstop, horrible shriek of what sounded like scratching, stretching, or bending metal. It was like some morbid underscore for an Alfred Hitchcock psycho-thriller . . . only worse. It was unnerving then, and I still cringe at the thought of it. It would be years before I could communicate that sound without complete withdrawal.

The windows were shaking, and glass exploded from everywhere. Those gorgeous natural wood-grained desks, chairs, and symbols of status went right out the window, literally. They violently and in succession freed themselves through our once sealed and priv-ileged views. Impositions of air whistled in whirlwinds and stole all that remained of usable air. Panic was instantaneous.

Unintelligible conversations familiar to the concourse now intruded on office decorum. I heard crying from every direction—from behind walls, underneath desks and tables, and even open corners. Most peculiar were the almost inaudible whimpers from behind elevator doors.

> "It was a bomb," someone called. The floor began buckling.

"It was a bomb," someone called. The floor began buck-ling. "Get out! Get out." "The building is coming down!" someone else shouted. It was only seconds before the mad dash toward the exits began.

I turned to my assistant. The place where she sat was empty. I turned again and watched her trembling body run for the exit while mine stood motionless at that window, paralyzed by the once beautiful sight of the sky. I stood there listening to debris falling from above, banging against the sides of the building, and filling the sky with all sizes of shredded paper, stone, furniture, and people. It was the ugliest and the most dreadful thing I had ever witnessed.

My mind tried desperately to find words my heart could understand. I didn't know anything in that moment . . . I couldn't speak. I couldn't think. All I could do was stand there. It was like watching a snowstorm with all sizes of weird and distorted flakes, burying me. It was like a blizzard, or a parade. It was confusing and obvious, and terrifying and breathtaking . . . all at once. It was . . . it was gray confetti . . . almost. I was lost in those moments.

Then almost in slow motion, that beautiful blue sky choked to death on a horrible smoke that filled the air until outside the window was nothing more than a gigantic dark gathering place for lost souls.

My heart stopped.

A rush of adrenaline shot up through me. I felt as if I had run a marathon or twenty miles uphill. My heart pounded so hard that it hurt. My breath was short and quick. I felt lightheaded—like I was suffocating. I watched things fall off the desks, I think. I think. . . .

Wet. Warm and wet. Urine ran down the side of my leg when someone shouted, "The ceiling is caving." I felt anxious. Then I heard moaning. It was too close for it to have been anyone but me. I grabbed my arm and told myself to move . . . move . . . move . . . Leslie.

My knees were weak beneath me. My legs struggled just to keep standing. My mind could not process what I wanted my body to do. My fingers tingled, and my heart leaped through my chest. My mouth was dry. My lips sealed. It felt like the floor had already begun to give way. Was it really sinking? I was queasy and overwhelmed by a feeling that I had never felt before. Whatever it was, it formed a scream that started deep inside my belly. It was big and bottomless and I could feel it growing—getting bigger, until it was bigger than the objects falling outside the windows. It tunneled through me . . . and then . . . stopped at my lips.

I felt very strange, detached from myself. I looked at my hands and my arms. I saw them, but I didn't really see them. They didn't look familiar. My legs looked fake. I couldn't figure them out. I thought, "What the . . . these aren't my hands. . . . This isn't me." I want to say that it was then that I moved toward the open windows . . . but I can't be sure. I heard myself talking, but my voice was inside my chest and pounding through some long tunnel. My words seemed muffled. I remember now that I kept making sounds, trying to hear "me." I was so removed, nothing seemed real. I felt discombobulated, like I was . . . I was floating . . . apart from everything . . . unattached . . . distant . . . lost.

> Then all of a sudden, I felt nothing. My body went completely numb.

Then all of a sudden, I felt nothing. My body went completely numb.

I walked zombie-like into my office and picked up the telephone. I wanted to call my cousin Ronnie. I'm not sure why. He's a smart man. Maybe I wanted him to explain all of this to me. He's strong, fearless, and protective. Maybe I thought he could defend me from whatever it was that was attacking me. He loved me. Maybe he could stop the pain. I needed to find some control somewhere and maybe, just maybe, I could somehow return the morning to normalcy or steal courage through his voice. Whatever the reason, I tried dialing him, but the connection failed.

The building swayed again and then settled. Looking back, it never really righted itself again. I hung up the phone and redialed.

From the corner of my eye, I could see frantic colleagues running in all directions, cussing and screaming. Again, someone shouted to me, "Leslie, what the [expletive] are you doing? Get the [expletive] out of here. This [expletive] building is coming down." I calmly hung up the phone and left my office. I left my life.

The journey began.

Hear my cry for mercy as I call to you for help, as I lift up my hands toward your Most Holy Place. Do not drag me away with the wicked, with those who do evil, who speak cordially with their neighbors but harbor malice in their hearts. Repay them for their deeds and for their evil work; repay them for what their hands have done and bring back upon them what they deserve. (Psalm 28:2–4)

CHAPTER 6

Step-by-Step

Deeper Into Darkness

Journal Entry

October 16, 2001

Ariella wants me to start journaling. I guess it's supposed to help me "process" . . . yea right. That's Ronnie's thing . . . not mine . . . and he's crazier than I am! Anyway, invisible friend, my therapy moves to New Paltz today . . . Ariella won't be coming here to talk anymore. Yippee. Yippee. I'm going to tell her that the Prozac makes me feel funny. I hate it. We're supposed to start EMDR today. She wants to know if I'm ready . . . that's stupid. Of course I'm not ready. I'm never ready. I don't know why she keeps pushing this EMDR stuff. Nothing's gonna help—especially not tapping my legs while I talk. She's a good therapist though. I like her. Never thought I'd be talking to one though. I probably needed to a long time ago.

I'm not so sure she really gets it. She wants me to take her there in my mind, but I'd rather NOT!!!! Get over it. Get over it. Get over it. I know that's what everybody thinks I should do . . . but I should feel this for the rest of my life. I would laugh if this whole thing weren't so pathetic and sad. . . . I can't even think straight anymore. I'm just gonna walk in there today and tell her to shove all of her degrees and pills and everything else . . . MS goody . . . goody. Somebody please help me . . . please please please please. I'm not ready to die!

God??? I need to be back by 2:30. Eliot gets home and . . . I hate this!!! I hate this whole thing!!!!!!—Even writing in this stupid book!!

I noticed Steve, the underwriting director, running toward the exit with something tucked underneath his arm. He looked at me as he passed. It was odd seeing him run like that. He had a look on his face as if he was going to be sick. Mary Alice was behind him. She was screaming and cussing for everybody to get out of the building.

The office became more and more deserted as the seconds ticked by. The smoke got thicker, and people were just running to get away. The explosions were so loud and so threatening. There were no distractions or independent course of action in what we were doing. We wanted out, and nobody stopped to try to figure things out or pick up anything that was dropped. Most left behind keys, jackets, purses. . . .

We left our lives.

Bhranti, a soft-spoken and always pleasant underwriting assistant, sat at her desk redressing her feet with walking shoes. She sat amidst her many family photos, and her eyes traveled quickly between the now emptying office and pictures of her children, weddings, birthdays, and family "fun" shots. Her eyes lifted as I approached her desk. She drew her lips away from her teeth in a narrow, insecure smile. I watched her composure change in her shaking hands. Looking back, I can only imagine what her thoughts must have been.

I waited for her, and we walked calmly toward the exit as if this mass exodus were a normal or expected occurrence. I noticed Bhranti glance back. Neither of us considered the gravity of our situation, nor did we speak of it. It seemed safer not to. Instead, our words blended until our conversation knotted into a bland and dull monologue. "Good morning,

> We were of like minds on autopilot, able to see and understand only the exit signs and following the crowd.

Bhranti." "Hi, Leslie . . . what happened?" "I don't know . . . maybe an earthquake." "Ha ha ha . . . an earthquake . . . wow . . . is Millie still in the bathroom?" "I don't think so." "Do you think I should bring my purse?" "Nah, it should be okay."

It went something like that, only more like chatter. We were of like minds on autopilot, able to see and understand only the exit signs and following the crowd. Again she glanced back. We never imagined that we would not return to our office. It was never a thought in our moments of bewilderment and forced exit that the city beneath us was in total chaos and suffering through a marriage of vulnerability and horror.

We had no idea that directly above us a plane had crashed into the building, leaving hundreds already dead and countless others praying for last rites. On impact, and just a few floors up from where we had sat seconds before, some of our colleagues had already been snatched from their seats and tossed like rag dolls into the open sky. My friends were hanging on to thin windowsills and making phone calls to say good-bye to their families. Lives interrupted.

Hundreds of would-be evacuees were desperately searching for acceptable escape routes, digging holes through walls, racing through corridors, and transferring from one stairway to another to avoid the large holes where floors were missing or in flames.

I had never seen fire so angry.

As we approached the central stairwell, the ceiling started to collapse into the reception area. An explosion forced fire through closed elevators doors with an angry swoosh, and the screaming metal sound got louder. I had never seen fire so angry. I never knew it was so loud. The crackling alone was deafening.

The cries that came from behind the twisted metal of bleeding elevator doors pierced my brain. People plunged to their deaths when cables melted from the heat. Others trapped in those suffocating lifts burned to death as flames shot down broken shafts. The sounds were bone-chilling.

I think Bhranti finally associated the sounds with what was happening, because she started to come unglued.

"It's okay, Bhranti. We'll be fine," I said, still on autopilot and still with no cognizant thoughts. I think I heard myself speak. I think I believed what I said.

There was only one exit available to us. We waited a few minutes until there was room enough for us to enter. It was a long, dark, and narrow stairway that we, like the others before us, forced our way into single file. There was only enough space for two people per step. So crammed and desperate, we walked like tightly wound robots—stiff and unresponsive, down stairs that led only deeper into the inconceivable. Every face carried a blank look, absent from its body.

At first there was an eerie silence in those stairs—a stillness with a quiet adrenaline and uneasy calmness that was really too calm. I noticed every infinitesimal detail, and my awareness followed every sound closely. The anxiety I felt isolated every footstep and amplified every breath. Every pant and every heartrending whimper etched in my mind.

Picture this. The stairwell was more like a movie set. The lighting, probably coming from emergency generators, was sparse and dim to none. It somehow stretched down the stairs and gave notice to moisture that settled on the scuffed and now smoke-stained walls. Dingy water dripped from busted pipes and through breaks in the cement ceilings, creating a constant flow down already slick stairs. The sound echoed. The railings—warm and covered by chipped metal paint—were lined with hands of all colors, like an assembly line.

The heat was insufferable, and the smell of the smoke was horrible—rancid. This was no ordinary smoke. It smelled of chemicals, rusted metal, and burning hair; fabric, flesh, inconceivable things. This was powerful, pungent, and fuel-saturated. It was thick and acidic, and burned badly in our throats and eyes, tingled on our skin.

Corporately, our thoughts were of surviving, so we pressed through it all. We descended slowly and stopped at almost every landing to make room for others entering the stairs. Slower still we moved to the left or to the right to accommodate the injured or avoid large puddles and holes.

At one point, there was a woman burned to the bone. It is mind-blowing to see how thin and sensitive skin really is. I could actually see the ivory marrow. We tried not to stare. But as she passed, tears rolled and mouths fell open. "Oh, my God," I heard someone say. The burned woman trembled uncontrollably. What was left of her flesh looked like it had been boiled. It was actually slipping off her body . . . just hanging there . . . loose. She was in total shock. Her arms were stiff and stretched out in front of her as if she were imitating a sleepwalker. Her escort held her very gently and led her down the stairs. She never looked at a soul.

What kind of motherless soul can so easily and savagely murder thousands and proclaim it all to be in the name of righteousness? What kind of righteousness annihilates lives with such contempt and in such grand scope that it leaves an entire world in mourning? This woman had a life.

A few flights down, I guess near the twenty-seventh floor, an Asian man positioned himself at the entrance of his office. He was clearly terrified, and he yelled for us to leave the stairs. He and his colleague ran back and forth from an open window to the stairs, as if measuring the degree of devastation from one place to the other.

He yelled that he had heard of fires beneath us and that it was too dangerous to continue downward. He suggested, no, urged us to join him and his colleague and wait for help.

Neither he nor I really knew what was ahead. I stared at him through my burning eyes and considered accepting his offer. He stared back nervously. I started to move toward him, but the momentum from the crowd behind pushed me on. I had no choice but to go with the flow. I followed.

Uncertainty is that seamless monster of polarity that obliterates us all. There was no sure way to go and no clear answers. There were no fire alarms, sirens, or signals to warn us of what lay ahead. Fear was our god, confusion our master, and we—those "fortunate" enough to be packed in the stairwell—were bound together by *that* god, descending deeper and deeper into the unknown, the arms of a waiting enemy we could not see.

> There was no sure way to go and no clear answers.

Somewhere about the twenty-fifth floor, and after several halts in our descent, a woman began to cry. It had a rippling effect. First one, then another, until before long the sounds of weeping women raced up the stairs faster than we could go down. Their cries sparked conversations and speculations that incited more fear.

I believe there is no worse predicament than the union of ignorance and peril. Somehow, seeing and knowing your enemy gives a little more hope. This was hopeless. My heart pounded faster and harder in my chest.

As more speculation entered, all rational thought exited. Rumor suggested that a *small* airplane had "accidentally" crashed into the building. Others said it was an earthquake, and, of course, some swore it was a bomb. We had no idea against what or whom we were fighting.

Whatever we did see and endure in those stairs, we were the lucky ones. For some, there were no stairs and no exit at all.

As more people filed into the stairwell, so did more hearsay and more tales of horror and narrowly averted disaster. There were hundreds of people before us and still hundreds more behind us, all of them in a frenzied passion, wanting to live to tell their story.

Flight after agonizing flight I listened to conjecture, wailing, and the "what-ifs" and "could-haves." Flight after torturous flight I heard the cries of tormented victims trapped and warning of something fierce, daunting, and unspeakable catching up to us.

> I could easily have just died and gone to heaven, had I not been bound for hell.

I think I was afraid. I know I was outside of myself. At that point, I could easily have just died and gone to heaven, had I not been bound for hell. Swallowing, I closed my eyes, and for the first time since the day began, I reached for my mother's legacy and prayed: "God, help us"—three words, three simple words that made all the difference in the world; three words that changed the course and consequences of my entire life, because they changed me.

I often wonder how many prayers flooded the gates of heaven that day. How many Christians, or otherwise, called on the Lord? How many Jews looked for the Almighty? How many others called, by whatever name, on the one true God? How many nonbelievers, if only for a moment, and if only to ask *how* this could happen, believed in Him and called on His name: "Jesus"?

I MET MICHAEL WHEN I worked for the Bank of New York. I was moving on to bigger and much better things, so I hired and trained him to take my place. He was smart, funny, and very cute. He had big bright eyes, dimpled cheeks, and a smile that made inquiring minds want to know more. Mike was a sharp dresser, sharper still in wit. He learned to do the job quickly. He learned to do the people immediately. After about a week, I found out that he knew the shortcuts of the job and already was making his own rules. Most days he spent more time socializing and warming up to the women than he did working. Nobody really cared because he really was a delightful man, and that was his way of getting things done. He could convince someone to take responsibility for certain aspects of his workload and have them think it was their own brilliant idea. That was Mike.

I got such a big kick out of him. He was easy to be around, and he could make me laugh until I bent over. His sense of humor, his love of life, and his gift for living each moment like it was his last endeared him to me. Few promises and fewer regrets.

In October 2001, I learned that Michael had lived his last moments a few floors above my head at Cantor Fitzgerald, in the World Trade Center's north tower, on September 11, 2001.

I bet he was brave.

I miss him.

PART TWO

The Enemy of My Enemy

CHAPTER 7

Strike Two

From Panic to Pandemonium

We continued our descent down the stairs. We kept on through the dark and bottomless depths of a maniac's loathing of religious freedoms—*nothing personal*. We kept finding something different behind every door we opened. While most of what we found was abandoned space, other spaces still sheltered people who were afraid to leave.

Another floor—another man peering out and more petrified people.

My cell phone rang. "Hello," I said—no response—"Service unavailable at this time." I swore.

As the minutes passed, the fumes became more intense. As we got closer to the bottom, my eyes burned more. Even with my lids shut. Bhranti, who was still walking next to me, also complained about her eyes and not being able to see or breathe. I noticed others removing their shirts and blouses so I took one from my bag. Still today, I can't tell you why I had my empty laptop bag or how the recently purchased blouse got there. I placed it over Bhranti's face and told her to take slow breaths. She did so unwillingly and then asked about me and my asthma. But my asthma was not a problem because in that moment and the moments that would follow, it was not a consideration and not a threat. The Holy Spirit breathed on my behalf.

I'm guessing that about the twentieth floor is where it happened. The heat was making me tired and I wanted to regroup. We stopped for a minute and someone opened another door. Unwittingly, I stuck my head in for cleaner air and there he was.

A man stood staring. It was a cold and blank look. He said nothing; trapped behind what once was probably a wall, his stare mesmerized me. I remember it being a mindless gaze with complete shock occupying the part of his flesh where his face used to be. There was no fire or smoke near him. Just huge chunks of broken glass, mangled and exposed wires out of their places, furniture upside down, cables and pieces of the wall lay everywhere.

Both large and small fragments of glass and other objects pierced the once perfectly papered walls. Crashes of more devastation howled from somewhere on that floor and the recognizable vociferous crackle of fire. I examined him closely from the stairs. His face . . . contorted like abstract art. His eyes . . . fixed on nothing. His mouth was wide and silent. His head rested between two small columns while his body was crooked and oddly twisted off to the side. He had been decapitated.

I think I shook my head in disbelief. I had never seen so fierce a death! Was I dreaming? Was this something my mind had conjured up? I wanted desperately to understand what I was seeing, or not seeing, but I couldn't.

"Close the door. Don't look," someone yelled, and the door slammed shut.

If only it had been that simple. If only it were possible to see merely with our eyes.

We see with our hearts. Our eyes are simply catalysts that carry images. Our eyes capture flowers and our heart knows serenity. Our eyes capture a child at play and our heart knows joy. They capture beauty and we know love. They capture war and we are acquainted with mortality. My eyes captured hatred and suffering, and my heart knew sorrow. They captured death and destruction and my heart knew fear. To close one door simply captured what was on the other side, and my heart broke more.

Linda, another underwriting assistant, was about one flight up and crying uncontrollably. I stood to the side of the stairs, letting others pass, and waited for her. I put my arm around her shoulder, trying to reassure her that we would be okay. I told her that we had no time to cry. "When we get out of this mess," I said in a small voice, "we'll cry together. But for now, we have to keep our eyes clear and we have to keep moving."

> My eyes captured hatred and suffering, and my heart knew sorrow.

She nodded. Then through moderately controlled tears, and getting more emotional as she spoke, Linda said that she had been in the World Trade Center during the 1993 bombing. She told me about her nightmares and her long road to recovery. She spoke about her doubts concerning survival, and with a mind-numbing regularity that in some way made her burden lighter she told me that she could not do "this" again.

I hardly heard a word she said. I looked right through her, kept my eyes on those ahead, and kept us both moving.

Still another flight . . . maybe the seventeenth floor . . . and once again, the crowd stopped moving. We were prisoners of yet another wretched moment. I hated those long pauses more than almost anything else that happened there. It was in those moments that every victim was *heard* and every prayer got louder. The alternative silence was much too loud and much too much to bear.

Further down, there were wails of "Oh, Jesus, Jesus" and "Help me, I don't wanna die." There were horrible shouts of "No" and "Please" and "Somebody, help us." Each plea pierced my faith a little more, seized my heart, and fear stole away my breath.

Even worse were the familiar voices of old cigarette buddies, elevator friends, and passing acquaintances—all calling out, all asking why, and all recognizable enough to make us wonder about colleagues or look down the stairs for friends. I think we all paused individually from time to time and hoped for those who we knew were in the building but we didn't see. We were powerless to help.

> One minute I was in
> the stairs and the
> next was . . .
> oblivion.

I'm not sure just when it happened, but somewhere around the ninth floor I noticed that the screams and the bangs, the explosions, and the grinding metal all blended into one constant and excruciating opus as panic escalated to pandemonium when the building suddenly rocked again.

One minute I was in the stairs and the next was . . . oblivion. With heart pounding, lungs contracting, eyes expanded to the size of my face, and drenched in a cold sweat, for one terrible and seemingly endless second, I was sure—positive—that I was dying. Absolute fear. It was full-blown disorientation and a whirlwind of nauseating terror.

LORNA, ONE OF MY COMMUTER "regulars," *worked in the World Financial Center directly across from the towers. She was at her desk and going about her morning as she normally would, when everything changed.*

"I glanced up and out the window because I heard an explosion. I thought at first that a bomb had gone off somewhere. Then somebody said a plane had hit Tower One.

"I saw [the second] plane heading straight for my building. I froze. Then I screamed. I watched the airplane turn on its side and raise a few feet, change directions . . . almost a complete turn . . . then back to its side and straight into the side of the [tower]. There was fire and smoke everywhere. I fell to my knees, and all I could see was this huge hole in the side of the building with fire shooting out of it. I just knew we were next, so everybody started running and screaming. That's when I saw the first body fall."

nside Tower One, the stairs shook more and flights collapsed. People slipped and stumbled. Linda fell into my back . . . heels first.

"What's happening? What's happening?" was the unison cry. Someone hollered up to us that the final exit door had slammed shut and was jammed. Something else was yelled. People cussed and then screamed and then . . . nothing. We just stood there, still and quiet for what seemed to be an eternity while every prisoner in that darkened and miserable staircase joined in immeasurable sorrow for what seemed to be our certain destiny.

Outside, the city held its breath in horror, staring into a black hole that was once a breathtaking landscape. Tower One stood strong, just smoking.

Inside, more jagged edges, more fires spread, more smoke made it harder to breathe. Explosions undoubtedly sealed more exits, trapped more people, and it became increasingly difficult to tell if we were still alive.

Just breathe, Leslie . . . just breathe.

It was just after nine, and Tower Two had been struck.

Silence washed over me. I felt weak.

CHAPTER 8

Exit Center

Angels in Our Midst

He who dwells in the secret place of the
Most High shall abide under the shadow of
the Almighty. I will say of the Lord, ''He is
my refuge and my fortress; My God, in Him I
will trust.'' Surely He shall deliver you from
the snare of the fowler and from the
perilous pestilence.

—PSALM 91:1–3 NKJV

As a child, I was precocious and often called a free spirit. I was
an active little girl with an honest zeal for life. Challenging rules
came very naturally.

Frequently sick from asthma, I was supposed to live under certain limitations. Instead, I would climb trees or play football with the
boys and then spend hours on my mother's lap trying to breathe
normally again. Although I couldn't articulate it at the time, I under-

stood the fragility of breath. I respected life and honored its Giver.

Even back then I was writing poems and having long conversations with the Lord. Before I really knew about the spiritual realm, I was having dreams and visions and was in touch with what we called "it." Being spiritual was my norm . . . it was who I was.

In my early years, it was my mother who told me that God would do mighty things in my life one day. But it was God who assured me that He would always be with me. My parents said my connectedness was a gift—a divine experience and a powerful spiritual connection with my heavenly Father. As I grew older and wanted to fellowship outside the church, I felt more isolated, more resentful, and more like it was a curse. I wanted out—all the way out.

In retrospect, in that blocked stairwell I wished for some leverage or bargaining tool with God. And in spite of it all, I think I sensed that He was there with me. Still, I stood there yielded to doom and trapped on the brink of hell; once again, like that little girl I once was, feeling isolated, cursed, and wanting out—all the way out.

There was a small tremor. It lasted only a few seconds but I guess it caused the building to twist more because some doors that were previously open, slammed and jammed shut.

A man yelled that perhaps we should turn around and head back up to see if we could transfer to another stairwell.

You shall not be afraid of the terror by night, nor of the arrow that flies by day, nor of the pestilence that walks in darkness, nor of the destruction that lays waste at noonday. A thousand may fall at your side, and ten thousand at your right hand; but it shall not come near you. Only with your eyes shall you look, and see the reward of the wicked. (Psalm 91:5–8 NKJV)

Looking back, there were no words at that moment and still none now to describe that trancelike feeling of being "over." None to relate that once-in-a-lifetime clarity of purpose and the realization that I had failed to fulfill mine. Trust me, there is nothing more miserable than the fear of dying and leaving so much undone and even more unspoken.

> There is nothing more miserable than the fear of dying and leaving so much undone and even more unspoken.

Not only was I full of repentance, I believe I reached a place where I understood that all the simple things we fight, scream, and complain about mean absolutely nothing. I was clear that all the "stuff" we work so hard to accumulate is temporary . . . of no real value. I got it. Life is a love story. I saw. I understood. It was clear. I was clear. That was how life "flashed" before my eyes, in clarity. It was a long pause of lucidity.

And then . . . then I gave up. I think we all did.

Suddenly and as unexpectedly as the exit door had closed and jammed, it opened and light trickled in. People pushed a little harder. This time the slightly anxious push became a frenzied shove toward the light. At last we had reached the lobby.

Water was everywhere. My eyes fixated on it as I tried to make out its discoloration. It was slightly red and deep. It was sluggish and did not flow willingly. The sharp odor of fuel emanated from it and took me back to the dripping I had heard earlier. This was it. This was where the water, fuel, and what appeared to be blood had found a place to collect our lives before completely draining us. We were ankle deep and plodding through it. My toes curled and tried to find a place in my shoes that was not touched by that dreadful puddle. Some women removed their shoes completely.

> Now go, lead the people to the place I spoke of, and my angel will go before you. (Exodus 32:34)

A somewhat tall man with a quiet smile held the exit door open and directed evacuees to the next and final exit. He looked serene. An aura, as I know it now, was around him. At the time, I had few thoughts about him except that he felt safe and that I wanted to be where he was.

Hopeless and lost, I lifted my eyes to the only place I knew where I could find peace.

I paused near him, leaned by the door, and watched as he directed others from the stairs. I wanted to stay there with him. His presence was comforting. He looked at me and smiled. He spoke to me very clearly. He told me to move on . . . that I couldn't stay there and that I would be okay. I believed him. His was the only smile I saw all day, and in that smile was the one place I saw faith.

It was perfect. It was reassuring. It was celestial.

Reluctantly, I moved on. I believe I exited the stairs at the plaza level but barely recognized it. No more was the concourse aglow with life. There were no sounds of hurried feet, rustling newspapers, or laughter and morning gibberish. Its voice now was the crackle of fire and random explosions. From every angle, it was crushed and dying, slightly grayed from smoke, defeated, crumbling, and slaughtered by glass bullets of injustice. Death absolutely reigned.

The smell was overpowering, and my lungs struggled frantically to blow out the stench of it. Then finally, hopeless and lost, I lifted my eyes to the only place I knew where I could find peace. *Hear my cry, O God, attend unto my prayer.*

I looked below me. Where had all the people gone? The officials who stood proudly every morning at the security stations had deserted them. Where were the masses that crowded the stairs? Other than those now pushing past me, the area was deserted and devoid of life.

I heard sirens coming from outside but saw no arriving knights in shining armor; at least not where I stood. There was some activity coming from the southern end of the building near the elevator banks. My eyes and subsequently my body followed the movement. I never really "saw" what was going on because my eyes stopped short of motion and focused on a very large glowing red object just outside the building. It lay near where the sculpture was supposed to be.

I stood near a railing and watched it glow, completely engrossed by the flames. There was something so frightening and magnificent about it that I couldn't pull myself away. Whatever it was, it affected me. I just stood there with my heart beating out of my chest, afraid to breathe in more of death's stench . . . or breathe out, as it might have been my last. My hands sweat and my knees buckled. I took a deep breath.

A woman stood beside me biting her arms in frustration. She was jumping up and down and banging her head between her hands. She was disheveled and wearing only one shoe. The other one was probably lost in that puddle. Between pauses in biting herself, she swore and yelled the same thing over and over again.

> # This part is hard to explain. It was composed chaos.

This part is hard to explain. It was composed chaos. People were running frantically trying to get away from the explosions and the flames. One man ran by us. I think he called us fools and shouted for us to move on. He was bleeding from his shoulder. Another one followed not far behind and ran by us yelling, "Get out of my way . . . get out of my way." Without being fully aware and without knowing why, I started *back* toward the stairs.

> In the morning you will say, "If only it were evening!" and in the evening, "If only it were morning!"—because of the terror that will fill your hearts and the sights that your eyes will see. (Deuteronomy 28:67)

I LOST MY VIRGINITY TO A stranger at fifteen years old. I was a popular high school sophomore with the personality of a cheerleader. I had more social engagements than homework assignments, and my many extracurricular activities afforded me more than reliable excuses to sneak away from school with friends.

One evening on my walk home at dusk, a gun and the cold hands of a stranger introduced me to the bitter truth about the evil that lurks in the hearts of man. Brutal thievery forced my body to a place reserved for those in love and left me angry and confused. I let go of all fantasies about first loves. All future intimate moments of sweet surrender were lost forever in the ugliness of a .32-caliber revolver, beer breath, and cheap cologne.

Years passed before I understood the nature of sex crimes and managed to let go of the bitterness. I came to understand the detachment of it all and I finally found some truths in my experience. I learned to count it all joy, like my father often said. I learned and believed that the gift of love is the one universal certainty of any significance to God. I learned and knew that even in the worst of times, God's loving arms are outstretched and waiting to carry us through.

M ore than anything, I wish I could speak of joy that came through all the suffering on that particular September morning, but I cannot. There was none. However, in the greatest moments of desperation and overwhelming sorrow, God's loving and outstretched arms were waiting for my acceptance. I now know that His holy presence and peace called to me at every point of overwhelming despondency and paralyzing trepidation.

I know that the Lord walked with me through that concourse. *Yea, though I walk through the valley of the shadow of death . . .*

He held me as my head turned about quickly and my eyes scoped every inch of what remained. *I will fear no evil.*

It was another place entirely. It was surreal, like a 3-D movie; too gigantic and slow to participate in, yet too fast for retreat. I felt vulnerable and very mortal. *For thou art with me.*

Everything I saw broke my heart a little more. *Thy rod and thy staff they comfort me. . . . Surely goodness and mercy shall follow me all the days of my life: and I will dwell in the house of the Lord for ever.*

Amen.

CHAPTER 9

War Zone

Spiritual Wickedness

What I saw was more than humbling. It was completely and unequivocally self-stripping. This grand beauty that minutes before was strong and filled with magnificence and light was suddenly bare and broken. Shards of glass lay strewn beneath what once were beautiful walls of glass.

What remained of the glass revolving doors was red with bits and pieces of human flesh clinging to them. I was flabbergasted, but I kept moving. I walked around in a trance with others who, like me, were aware of what they saw but were unable to connect emotionally.

There were no flower planters or vendors outside the entrance anymore. Instead, there were chunks of broken stone, crushed benches, and huge peculiar objects glowing or still burning. There were fallen chandeliers and deserted security stations. There was no aroma of deli food or smell of maintenance, only fuel odor, piles of ash, and debris. All not burning, glowed with an intense heat. All not cut and weakened by a thousand jagged edges was not far from it. All that remained was desolation.

I covered my face with my hands and slowly bowed my head.

Movement caught my attention, and I looked up. It was then that I heard the scrambled radios and noticed police officers carrying victims and firefighters racing into the stairways. There they were—the cavalry—my knights.

One after the other those noble men ran toward the upper floors with little hope of survival and all the grace of God. They shouted to one another as they hurried about, and despite the distance between us, I saw dread in their faces. I saw years of training and rescue procedures boil down to that one moment. That moment that broke millions of hearts with a single falling tear or drop of blood heard from downtown New York City to the hills of California, the towers in Paris, and the deserts of Afghanistan.

> They began their climb upward and into the pages of history.

I believe the rescuers knew what was waiting for them up those stairs. Their eyes said so. I believe they knew they wouldn't return, and although there was no time for intense soul searching or contemplation, I saw them choose the ultimate sacrifice. I saw them! Radios ignored! Some with gear in hand and others with equipment resolutely unfastened and left behind; they began their climb upward and into the pages of history.

They tossed people down the stairs and to safety. They dragged bodies out of the way. They screamed, yelled, and shouted to us to keep moving. They scraped aside metal and glass. With bloodied fingers they moved obstacles while the Twins were getting beaten into total and complete surrender.

Put on the whole armour of God, that ye may be able to stand against the wiles of the devil. For we wrestle not against flesh and blood, but against principalities, against powers, against the rulers of the darkness of this world, against spiritual wickedness in high places. (Ephesians 6:11–12 KJV)

A large mound of something charred lay near the elevators. A woman, I think, lay near it. A small amount of blood was near her neck area. Her legs splayed out awkwardly, and her eyes were shut, but not completely; they had rolled back as if she was unconscious. Her arm lay to her side and her chest rose and dropped rapidly. She was panting.

I just stood there, watching, listening—and with every moment that passed, I lost a little bit more of the woman I was at 8:45 that morning. Every second that I stood breathing was a miracle, and each one confirmed for me my finite self.

Most of us have had "mystical" moments in one way or another. At some point in our lives we have had that feeling of déjà vu or dread in a premonition. We have found occasion to share unnatural stories about visions or of dreaming about gardens one night and then receiving flowers the next day. Sometimes we encounter experiences that are unexplainable or unattached to a particular person or event. These moments are easy enough to ignore, because our first instinct is to disbelieve what we cannot understand and discount what is unfamiliar to us.

But there are those rare circumstances in which there is a convergence of spiritual awareness, insight, and fulfillment, and one dreadful place is born or realized. Although to describe it as a place is ambiguous. It is no more a "place" than I am a "thing." It crosses that extreme and fine line between spiritual awareness and psychosis.

It is more accurately described as a resolute challenge to our limited and relative mind. It is a vast and incalculable core of awareness that goes beyond our tiny range of personal knowledge, experience, accountability, or understanding of space, time, self, familiarity, identity, and even reality. It is distinct, and it is the determination of the *now* we live in. Call it the spirit realm, imagination, hyperbole . . . or insanity. You may even write it off as enigmatic, but whatever it is, it is—was—the backdrop of my day and it was, without a doubt, linked to that inner place.

I wandered inside of myself . . .

. . . and there it was, the one "thing" that had called to me my entire life. That thing that had drawn me in for so long and kept me on the edge. That thing that made it impossible for me to walk dark halls or believe in "floating" molecules seen through my periphery. That thing that I never dared speak of . . . until now.

Never before had I dared to travel so deep inside of me to touch this "thing" or find this "place." I fail miserably even in describing my inability to describe it. Nevertheless, I am aware now of my finite self and infinite spirit. I am aware that beyond my flesh or inside of me and in each of us is a "place" where we war.

This is the place that resolves our lives and how victoriously or "defeatedly" we live them. This is "that place" where spirits dwell and linger and seek to destroy, and though we are equipped to fight we are not prepared. We lack understanding and walk superstitiously in fear and disbelief. But disbelief does not topple truth!

The real war.

I covered my face and was trying not to see anything more. I heard a voice. It told me to stand quietly and not to move. It whispered that my family would mourn me and pay dearly for all of the painful, lonely years that I had suffered. They would be sorry for the judgments I had endured at their hands. "They deserve your death." It spoke to me in an ominous but pitiful voice, so I responded. I stood motionless . . . readying myself for death . . . and . . . I listened.

Intense thoughts and emotions overcame me. My head was spinning. A tiny almost miniscule fiber connected my own will to my self-awareness. I couldn't separate visions from life occurrences, the dead from the dying, or the victims from the survivors.

Tiny rat-like shadows moved quickly around me. I watched myself vomit from the

> I couldn't separate visions from life occurrences, the dead from the dying, or the victims from the survivors.

taste of someone else's blood. The uniqueness of soured death was on my lips and his voice was in my ear. I smelled him and inhaled him I touched him, and in passing, he touched me.

> Wherefore take unto you the whole armour of God, that ye may be able to withstand in the evil day, and having done all, to stand. (Ephesians 6:13 KJV)

I read somewhere that in our human capacity it is difficult for our minds to remain alert to subtle things when there are so many macro events occurring around us. Too often we fail to see big lessons in small things because we are so preoccupied with the big things of little to no significance. This was, for me, such an occasion. *This is where I ended.*

I heard weeping as death erased all color lines and blinded eyes to cultural distinction. I saw hope forgotten as blade joined with flesh and left behind scattered traces of a single soul. Unidentifiable bloodless limbs and white bone fragments lay erratically scattered about once shining floors like uncollected trash.

With my head between my arms and my hands clasped behind my head, I started walking . . . with no certain course—just walking—slowly at first, scoping every inch of what I could see and getting more confused by what I didn't see—my enemy.

I saw fire so hot that in minutes concrete was ash; so arrogant that it dissolved thousands of years of segregation into one history. Indiscriminate, as still burning human torsos and unrecognizable charred human remains lay close enough to mounds of melting metal that they seemed to be one object. Glowing metal fused into concrete. It was incomprehensible.

With blatant dull thuds and pops of exploding flesh, persons once known as, became another of the unknown bodies twisted in midair and liberated from business attire, with legs pointed upward, arms spread eagle, and faces looking into the wind. Friends who once were, became vicious, newly created weapons of war and crashed into cement, mangled.

Shoes, hats, notes, pens, phone messages, cell phones, purses, combs, and all kinds of personal items lay about—abandoned in the escape or lost in the air. I gave in to despair.

Still-breathing masses leaped over terrors, disassociated, disoriented, and torn apart. There were trails of urine, blood, and other human waste evacuated in fear; spilled sporadically throughout the concourse. Both women and men curled up in corners too afraid or too given to shock to move. I felt my tower, as its steel bones began to break from the enormous burden, erupt in black vomit, with no pretense of dignity.

And yet, for me, the concourse gave witness to the spirit and compassionate presence of God. It was here that the most significant displays of courage and heroism took place.

I watched ordinary men and women clad in suits and dresses transform into heroes and carry others to safety. Some removed their jackets and used them to smother fire from the bloody, peeling bodies of strangers while others comforted those lost in shock.

> The concourse gave witness to the spirit and compassionate presence of God.

Ordinary people, who minutes before the first plane left Logan Airport in Boston sat typing, reading e-mails, and drinking coffee, were now desperately fighting for the heroic embrace of life.

I witnessed the tears of port authority and city police officers, now vulnerable, crying out to God as they bravely tried to maintain a hasty and orderly evacuation, despite the circumstances and no matter the severity. In those moments, there seemed to be no justice.

For a while I just stood there, very still and very quiet. My brain was unable to wrap itself around what was happening—still listening to the voices. I think somehow I believed that if I avoided movement, I would also avoid the inevitable. I would be invisible to death's grip. As I continued to watch, my eyes captured every devastating minute, and my heart stopped.

10 Seconds to Fall

"10"—I close my eyes and kiss the skies
To dream of a place where I can fly
"9"—I spread my wings until it seems . . .
that I'm a child again
"8"—I believed in angels and life was good
When
they laid me down to sleep
I prayed for promises
and streets of gold
If alas they came to keep my soul
"7"—I wonder now . . . so high on life that death intoxicates
me . . .
And as I dance . . .
entranced
on eyelids of twins
and sing . . .
of wings
and heavenly places
   I know
      I'm still
"6"—100 stories above the earth . . . and my own is just a whisper
Ashes to the same ashes that once birthed me
I see,
my return

so near to God that I feel His breath
so far from Him,
I pray He sees

Me . . .

and the truth
"5"—I stretch out my hand and reach for it . . .
The truth that is—I'll grab it,
The way that is—I'll hold it,
The light that shines—now grows,

Bold

And oh . . .

so

strong

Till it becomes

my faith
And it . . . faith . . .
will save me. . . .
"Yes"
"4"—From the angry fire behind me . . . that spits when he
laughs
The heat inside me . . . that burns when I cry
The pain around me . . . that smothers my soul . . .
and then
me
Until I no longer breathe
"3"—I close my eyes and kiss the skies and an angel meets me
here

Already at . . .
"2"—
He holds my hand and hums the song my mama sang to the crib
Not long enough ago
When dreams
were smiles and peaceful grins,
and twins
were people
I close my eyes and kiss the skies and gravity gives way
I spread my wings until it seems I am born again
"1"—and then,
    Sin
    Is erased
    and I hear a name
    Sweet Jesus . . .
    It's mine
    sung with "hal—le—lu-jah"
    and blended with cold cement . . .
    Amen.
    Amen.

CHAPTER 10

The Birth of Inspiration

The End of Me

I wandered around that concourse for the rest of my life. I stumbled in circles for what seemed an eternity—walking from one corner to the next trying to figure my way out. Distracted by people lost to themselves in the fetal position on the floor, I lost my way a few times.

Even more confusing was the sea of bloodied blue shirts as I tried to make my way out. Looking back, I believe it was in those moments that I collected the pieces of who I would later become.

This is hard to write. My stomach aches now as it did then.

I remember being struck by something so hard that it knocked the wind from me. I was later told that it was an exploded torso that had projected a few feet and hit me. I was told that I just looked down and then just stepped over it.

I don't remember clearly the exact details of this incident, but I do remember feeling responsible. I felt that it was only a matter of time before I too was lying on the floor somewhere—gone. I stood very still and waited . . . for death . . . even if it meant being gutted by one of those jagged edges that rained from the sky. I'm ashamed to say it now, but I wanted the agony of living to stop and to be immediately relieved of this burden too deep for words. I stared down, trying to avoid looking at those cold blank faces without names. My heart was in a frantic search for God. *How can I find you in the midst of all this?*

I walked away in sacrificial indifference.

DEAR MOM,

I sorry for the way I acted today, But I didn't mean it that way. It's just that last time I fell asleep watching this boring show and I almost threw up. I want to spend time with you but I also want to spend time with my friends and this "puberty" thing is really messing me up. So please forgive me for being mean.

Love Eliot

I gave birth to my only child when I was twenty-six years old. I experienced all the joys and pains of pregnancy largely on my own, and for the most part, I was alone when I gave birth.

There was no "love of my life" standing by my side and holding my hand. I had good friends there who stood with me all night and prayed with me before, and after, my son was born.

After seventy-two hours of waiting and praying and pushing, Eliot Cameron was born. He was 7 pounds, 14½ ounces of miracle! I read to him from the womb to the cradle and still now. I sang him to sleep and stroked his little face while he slept. I delighted in just the smell of his milky breath and bright morning eyes.

As Eliot learned to speak, we took turns telling bedtime stories about angels and toys. Toys were his favorite. He is the only good thing I have ever done, and unlike most teenagers, I like him. I liked who he was when he was three and talked to me about Jesus. I liked who he was at nine when he wrote the letter about being mean to me, I liked who he was at thirteen when this nightmare began, and I really like him now, at seventeen.

I watch him becoming a man. It is an amazing thing to see my little boy building a personal relationship with God—making our faith his own. He is a caring, secure, intelligent, and silly Allen Iverson wannabe, and he is NOT ashamed to be called a child of God.

Single parenting has not been easy, but it has been worth every minute of joy, pain, sickness, good grades, night fears, fevers, ear infections, birthday parties, and bellyaches. For years being Eliot's mom defined me. Seeing him smile was my motivation—what drove me. So it makes perfect sense that my first thought beyond the World Trade Center that morning was of my son and eleven years of Friday nights with pizza and a Blockbuster movie.

> My first thought beyond the World Trade Center that morning was of my son and eleven years of Friday nights with pizza and a Blockbuster movie.

I was not ready to give that up. I was not willing to go "quietly into the night" and say good-bye to Eliot. I wanted to go home!

As for you, you were dead in your transgressions and sins, in which you used to live when you followed the ways of this world and of the ruler of the kingdom of the air. . . . But because of his great love for us, God, who is rich in mercy, made us alive with Christ even when we were dead in transgressions—it is by grace you have been saved. (Ephesians 2:1–2, 4–5)

I saw small crowds hurrying toward the sky bridge that connected the World Trade Center to the Financial Towers, a complex of buildings behind the WTC. "This way, this way," someone called.

I turned toward the voices and saw a tall, thin man. At first, I didn't recognize what he was doing, but I'll never forget his eyes. They were hazel in color and full of panic. I realized he was on fire. His skin looked as if it was dissolving off his bones. Flames covered a large part of his body. He ran from the stairs and toward me. Another man was chasing him and hitting at him with his bare hands—trying to squelch the flames. I didn't even think to try to help.

I just stood out of the way, holding my chest in upset. Finally, somebody tackled the man with a jacket and put out the flames. He lay in front of me, motionless, smoldering. The skin on his face was burned black like toast. It looked like a bad Halloween mask.

The wide open space where I was standing was bright by now from the sun—an ironic contrast to the pitch black of where we really were.

There was sporadic activity here and there, but nothing that could have been called a planned evacuation. For years I have worked in office buildings that mandated fire drills. They would notify our staff twenty-four hours in advance so that we would be ready to respond. When the alarm sounded, everyone would line the walls outside their offices and wait for the "all clear"—usually no more than three minutes later.

At this point, even though intentions were good, I question the value of such a drill. In no way did years of lining the walls on command prepare for evacuating a mammoth tower set ablaze or deciphering procedures through the controlled chaos of yelling port authority police officers and firefighters; nobody knew how to remove tens of thousands of people from the blast radius of a triggered time bomb.

The random thumps that started shortly after the first jet hit were more frequent now. Body parts were everywhere. It was worse than watching a movie. I remember hearing myself, still outside myself, ask someone if all this was real. "Is this really happening?" I asked.

That's when he fell . . . or jumped.

I was standing closer to the sky bridge. The glass was morbidly stained by what is now my recurring nightmare. I'm not exactly sure why, but I froze there, just watching firemen watch the sky.

Even though I was told not to, I looked up and I saw his face. I don't know where his fall originated, but I watched him fall from probably the ninth floor until he hit the ground. I had no other choice.

He had dark blond hair and green eyes, which by the time I saw them were draining blood from their sockets. I must have been lost again in shock because my thoughts were not of his present state but of his morning routine. I wondered how long it took him to shave his face that morning and what he could have been thinking about as he dressed for work.

His light blue shirt and dark pants were classic office attire. I wondered what he did for a living.

The look on his face was one of surprise. I don't think he knew what was happening to him, at least that's the way I prefer to remember it. When he landed he was spread flat and staring up . . . no sound came from him. He wasn't screaming or crying at all.

I heard that at a speed of just less than one hundred fifty miles per hour, the fall lasted ten seconds—not fast enough to cause unconsciousness when falling, but slow enough to remain aware of one's final moments.

Just then a man, a firefighter I think, gently pushed me forward. "You can't stay here. It's not safe," he said. "Keep moving. Run."

Something snapped. And so I did. I ran.

I ran like I have never run before.

> I ran with no idea where I was running to, but with a crystal-clarity about the place I was running from.

Imagine being me. I ran without legs beneath me and with my heart pounding outside of my chest. I ran with no thought or question about why. I ran with no idea where I was running to, but with a crystal-clarity about the place I was running from. I ran with my arms shielding my head— through areas and scenes that I still do not recognize.

Others were running too; like the wind, swearing and screaming unintelligible words, like banshees.

In those few moments of flight, there might have been born . . . an epiphany. For some, death was the choice to fall or to fly. Others decidedly stood nearby for friends or for duty. In each case, death here was as affecting as life's last hurrah. But for me, it was the beginning. . . .

The Birth of Inspiration

I exited Tower One and left behind the pride in my career accomplishments, my arrogance, my power suits, power lunches, swollen ego, and self-righteousness.

This is where I was born.

CHAPTER II

Goliath Falls

The Beginnings of Sorrows

And when ye shall hear of wars and rumours of wars, be ye not troubled: for such things must needs be; but the end shall not be yet. For nation shall rise against nation, and kingdom against kingdom: and there shall be earthquakes in divers places, and there shall be famines and troubles: these are the beginnings of sorrows.

—MARK 13:7–8 KJV

WHAT SEPTEMBER MEANS TO ME . . . .

September . . . the first day of school and the promise of longer nights. Those were the days. How I love its eclectic smells, its sharpened pencils and chalked erasers against a blackboard eagerly waiting to record history—yeah, erasers. Those built–in chalk makers, fun makers and finders of new friends. School days, school days, those happy golden rule days—days of new clothes and school supplies—shuffling leaves—notebooks neatly divided into subjects never really discussed, and new shoes—new plans—long corridors and short bells, food fights, recess and banged up lockers—yeah. Youth . . . the fine lines of notebook paper and the smell—um yeah, new books, new friends and new bus routes. Ending summer romances, final farewells, barbeques and visiting relatives that stay too long. The beginning of the Christmas countdown and long letters that began "Dear Santa." Yeah, barbeque, that's September, bar-beque.

I noticed Millie, a member of my staff, on the sky bridge. She was alone, crying, and because of her weight and bad leg, struggling to keep going. I went over and kept her company until she was ready to start moving again. I'm not sure who supported whom, but with my arm wrapped around her shoulder, and her right hand in mine, we crossed the bridge.

Millie was in the World Trade Center during the 1993 bombing, and like Linda, she wanted to talk about it. So we talked about it. Correction, she talked. I kept us moving. The conversation was like the others I'd had that morning—one-sided and mindless. It went from the bombing to her having left her purse in the office and not knowing how she would get home, then back to the bombing. I nodded my head in acknowledgment and kept my focus straight ahead. I heard her but I had little idea what she was saying. My instincts were basic; keep moving and get out of the area.

From where we were on the bridge, I could see the atrium of the Financial Center and hundreds of evacuees and onlookers. They stood ogling and almost cheering for us as we approached.

A little more than halfway across, I noticed Nancy. She was an old commuter friend from years before. We rode the bus together, and my memories of her were fond ones. She was always polite and always smiling. A terrific conversationalist, Nancy was strong, decisive, and confident.

I hadn't seen her in more than two years and there she was. I caught her eye as she passed us. She was walking with someone as well—much in the same way that I was walking with Millie. She looked at me and for the first time in the many years I had known her, there was no laughter in her smile. Instead, I saw a woman with a forced nervous grin and a million questions in her eyes. I almost smiled politely, but I definitely shook my head. She shrugged her shoulders, I mine, and we continued the long crossing to the Financial Center and to safety.

I noticed immediately that the Financial Center's atrium was completely untouched. It was like entering the twilight zone—a parallel dimension with no signs of bereavement whatsoever. It was as beautiful as ever. Everything was in perfect placement. Its long marble staircase cascaded down into the area of tall palm trees that on many days was the perfect lunch spot. My first impulse was to sit for a minute on the benches surrounding the indoor garden and take a deep breath of resolution. But, twilight zone or not, I was still not close enough to home. And although the structure was untouched, the chaos was far-reaching. People were running everywhere. No one knew where to go. Millie and I moved slower now as we took it all in.

A woman ran by, obviously in shock. Her face was drenched—awash with tears and what looked like slobber. As she passed, she was praying aloud. She was running toward the plaza and crossing herself—running, crossing, saying prayers, kissing her fingers, running, and crossing. Believe it or not, it struck me as being funny.

Have you ever been so afraid that you lost all sense of . . . everything? I almost laughed at her. . . .

> Tragedy is a bizarre irony in that it can be fascinating, mesmerizing, and at the same time heart wrenching.

Millie and I walked down the stairs. We moved in a slow but deliberate purple haze. Just walking, watching, and saying nothing. Police officers and firefighters were still yelling. The urgency in their blaring at us catapulted me back into the grim reality of our location and made me fearful again. I was so shook up and confused that I was almost in tears. Had I even a vague idea of the enormity of what was still to come, I probably would have saved the tears for weeping and gnashing of teeth.

Crowds of people stood near the Financial Center exits. They stared with inviting eyes. I could tell that they wanted, no . . . needed, to hear the individual accounts of what it was like inside the Twins. They needed us to validate the savagery so that they could justify their hollering and then move on. But no one really moved on. Not from that . . . no one could. It was too hard to do that . . .

to let go . . . to walk away. It was too hard and still too surreal, you know.

Tragedy is a bizarre irony in that it can be fascinating, mesmerizing, and at the same time heart wrenching. For some, there is no escaping that carnal "need to know" or that compelling dark hunger to "spare no details." Therefore, although varying in the degrees of atrocity, we were all poets, and it was inevitable that eventually each of us would "spare few details" in telling our stories.

These things have I spoken unto you, that ye should not be offended. They shall put you out of the synagogues: yea, the time cometh, that whosoever killeth you will think that he doeth God service. And these things will they do unto you, because they have not known the Father, nor me. (John 16:1–3 KJV)

We exited at the far end of the building closest to where the Financial Center ferry docked. There an even bigger crowd lined the sidewalk and looked up at the burning towers. Some were talking, but most were in quiet repudiation . . . speechless. Groups hugged and tried to console one another. Most just stared up and cried.

Millie and I separated. I lost sight of her and never saw her again.

I drifted through the crowd for a while, until miraculously, I ran into Nancy again. By then the details of what really happened had begun to surface.

Witnesses saw two airplanes intentionally fly directly into both towers in an apparent terrorist attack. To us, this was just an assumption. How could it be anything other than an accident . . . how?

A West Indian woman, thick with her accent and heavy in her hands, stood near us shaking her body hysterically as if she were doing a dance. She pranced back and forth like a tiger, shouting "sabotage" and "terrorism." I could see that she was furious and scared at the same time. There were tears in her eyes and she kept balling her fists, taking short leaps into the air, and stamping her feet violently against the pavement as she landed. Because of her accent she lost me on some words, but I could plainly understand her demands for revenge.

Nancy and I gasped and shook our heads in disbelief. This was extreme. This was too much. On top of all the other stuff this day had vomited into our consciousness, this was much too much information to process. . . .

> We didn't know what to believe, so we discounted all of it.

We didn't know what to believe, so we discounted all of it. After all, it couldn't be true. This was America, New York, 2001. These things didn't happen to us, did they? We don't have terrorist attacks on this soil, do we? We don't nurture souls so black, with hatred so profound, as to exact such deliberate and ruthless slaughter on thousands of innocents . . . not anymore . . . not again, do we?

Nancy and I looked intently at each other, seeking confirmation that we had not gone completely mad. Someone behind us cursed terrorists and vowed vengeance on America's behalf. "This means war. This means war!" they cried. I lit a cigarette.

"Oh my—look, there goes another one." Nancy and I looked up, aghast at what we saw. Nancy shuddered. I told her that I had seen at least ten already. She gasped. For a second she looked queasy. We stood there . . . together . . . and watched one after another choose death by flight.

One couple stood close to the edge of a window, held hands, and let themselves go. I watched her dress opening and flapping in the wind almost birdlike. His suit rounded over his back in the wind as he fell. I imagined the sound of the air pushing past their ears and creating that low reverberation that you hear when you stick your head out a moving car window. I thought about how the wind can steal your breath away and how the pushing air vigorously massages the skin. Except for the end, it would have been exhilarating.

Their hands separated midair and they tumbled. Finally their bodies met with the hundreds who fell or were pushed or jumped before them. One by one, they landed—ending dreams, plans, futures, and families. I felt a soft moist hand close into mine. I heard a sigh deeper than the pains of a mother losing her only child. Nancy.

Bystanders shrieked in horror. They wondered aloud what terrible thing forced those people to those open windows. What vileness made human beings desperate to be volunteers? They couldn't imagine making that choice.

Meanwhile, those of us who survived that particular battle knew too well what went on behind those walls. We were well acquainted with the jagged edges and angry fire. We walked through the intense heat. It seared our own skin. We knew too well the brutal nature of mass murder. We knew of the thin ledge outside those windows that couldn't accommodate so many waiting for rescue—pushed. We knew of the explosions of flames that wipe out reason—jump. We were in accord with the severity of a reality so dreadful that it gave way to hopelessness—surrender. We too had been so afraid that we lost all sense of . . . everything.

I propose now, in hindsight, that in situations like these, it is neither necessary nor possible for us to understand all the whys or hows in order to learn from them. It is neither consequential nor probable to fully process these moments with a rational mind. They are too deep. We need only surrender that moment to the moment and leave "comprehension" or "meaning" to follow in the fullness of time . . . eternity.

This is the lesson: God is sovereign and though He allows us to live the consequences of our choices, He will assign meaning to our moments and redeem us. He is our Redeemer.

I watched more fall or jump. By now I was so removed that I couldn't even cry. Instead my mind made art of it all. I chose to go even further down that particular rabbit hole.

I noticed that as they fell their arms seemed like gliders waving calmly in the wind. I noticed the slow and steady motion of the fall itself, and again, I imagined the sounds and the whispers midair. Their clothing spread out like canopies in the gentle breeze of the once beautiful autumn air. How could something so stunning be so heartbreaking? I just looked, smoked my cigarettes, and counted.

I remember the color of his shirt . . .

"Leslie . . . Leslie . . . LESLIE." A sharp voice snatched me back. "Let's get away from here." It was Nancy. She grabbed my arm and we headed for a ferry. The ferry would take us back to Hoboken so that we could board a train going to upstate New York . . . home.

I realized that I only had a little cash. "Nancy, I need to find an ATM. I have no cash for the ferry." She looked at me with a question mark above her brow, undoubtedly wondering, *What are you talking about, Leslie?*

"We're not stopping, and we don't need tickets or money!" She kept her focus and kept walking, all the while tugging me closely behind her—like a mother pulling her child along—and sputtering about my being ridiculous. Our slow walk got faster as we got closer to the dock. Judging from the look on her face, that putrid taste of smoke was washed from her mouth by the taste of freedom. I guess she saw more than a boat.

Making a final attempt to process the day, I glanced over my shoulder one last time.

I looked back in risk—lest I become a pillar of salt—subconsciously knowing that that part of my life was over but wanting to hold on to it. I suspect that intuitively I knew I would never return to the Trade Center as it was. Maybe the masses that stood around knew something as well, and they mourned the towers long before they fell.

> I looked back in risk—
> lest I become a pillar
> of salt—subconsciously
> knowing that that
> part of my life was
> over. . . .

There was nothing left to me. Nothing except my instincts and a voice of anguish inside, fostering its relationship to every scream, every pop, thud, explosion, and moan that had replaced the quiet sips of my early morning coffee. We would soon be reconciled.

> Therefore in one day her plagues will overtake her: death, mourning and famine. She will be consumed by fire, for mighty is the Lord God who judges her. When the kings of the earth

who committed adultery with her and shared her luxury see the smoke of her burning, they will weep and mourn over her. Terrified at her torment, they will stand far off and cry: "Woe! Woe, O great city, O Babylon, city of power! In one hour your doom has come!" (Revelation 18:8–10)

Nancy and I reached the ferry dock. Again, I mentioned an ATM and cash. Again, she told me not to be ridiculous and pulled me along. We pushed our way through the crowd. Nancy was determined to get aboard and not to leave me behind.

There were so many people trying to get on that we were afraid there would not be enough room for us. Nancy pushed. It was probably her way of fighting back. She pushed hard, and while pulling me by the arm, we boarded the ferry. With perhaps one foot on the dock and the other on board, the boat pulled out—leaving behind hundreds of panic-stricken survivors and bystanders.

Not knowing if or when another ferry would come, they hung on to the railings near the dock, crying and begging us not to leave. All of them wanting . . . wanting their slippers, their favorite TV dinners and fish sticks and mothers and mothers-in-law and sodas and warm blankets and dogs and cats and credit card bills and old movies and repossession notices and . . . and loved ones and telephones and TVs and beds and just . . . simply . . . normal . . . home.

Nancy dropped my hand and walked toward the back of the boat.

I looked around. I didn't like being alone. Alone, I couldn't make sense of anything. I remember looking down at my feet and for some reason patting my toes in my shoes. I remember looking at the seats of the boat. They didn't make sense. The floor didn't look like a floor, and the people seemed . . . unreal.

THE BEGINNING — My parents, Larrystine and Willie Clark, at our home on Chicago's far south side. It's easy to see the distinction of my African heritage on my father's face. It's even easier to see the smile I inherited from my mom. No doubt, they were going to one of their many church functions because my mom is wearing one of her dress-up belts and my dad's in a suit. This picture was taken about 1979, before my mother's battle with cancer. She was beautiful even until her death in 1982. My father died shortly after her.

LAWRENCE AND ME — In my parents' front yard, on eighth-grade graduation day. I was 13 and my brother Lawrence was 16 and already starting to look after me.

ME AND MY SHADOW — "Young Master Eliot" was about 8 months old here. He was the most beautiful little bald baby I'd ever seen. I loved holding him up for the camera. This picture was taken outside of a church on a visit to Chicago. I miss those days!

LOVE AT FIRST SIGHT—
Monai and Eliot first met when she was 8
and he was 3. This was her first weekend
in our home. They fell in love immediately
and remain very close. To date, she still
lovingly calls him "the boy" and he calls
her "my sister."

MATERIALISTIC DAYS—
During my quest for more "stuff," I owned
about five mink coats. Honestly, beaver
doesn't suit me.

**UP THE CORPORATE
LADDER** — Early in my career I shared
an office with a male co-worker. I was on
the phone exerting some "girl power" when
someone took a picture. These were the
days of making the monster.

STILL HOLDING ON—
At Lawrence's house on a summer
visit to Chicago with him and his wife,
Sylvia. It drove him crazy that I was
such a nonconformist, so I often went
overboard with it...notice the jeans.

MY WEAKNESS — I took Eliot and Monai on a
much needed holiday in 2000 and visited Cedar Point
Amusement Park in Ohio. They're not in this photo, but
the important thing is...cotton candy!

MY SECURITY ACCESS — I kept my access
badge and business cards (and also my laptop bag)
so that my children's children would know that
Grandma was there. Lumbermen's Mutual was the
holding company for Kemper Insurance.

HASKIN
LESLIE D.
00
LUMBERMENS MUTUAL CAS

(Kemper.
Insurance Companies

Leslie D. Haskin
Branch Services Director

BUSINESS CUSTOMER GROUP

1 World Trade Center
36th Floor
New York, NY 10048-0637

(212) 313-4088
FAX (212) 313-4207

lhaskins@kemperinsurance.com
www.kemperinsurance.com

A WORLD APART — I used to love shopping and eating in the World Trade Center. This news photo is from 1979, six years after the towers officially opened. © AP Images

A GRAND WELCOME — Each morning soaring lobby windows and gleaming marble greeted me and thousands of WTC fans at the front door. This shot is taken from the plaza level. © Lawrence A. Martin / GreatBuildings.com

KNIGHT IN SHINING ARMOR — On that September morning, each stairwell varied in condition. Parts were gone altogether. This photo shows Engine 28 fire fighter Mike Kehoe helping in the evacuation of Tower One. The picture was taken by John Labriola, who had an office on the 71st floor. News reports said both he and Mike escaped with no injuries. © AP Images, John Labriola

DARKNESS CAME — After the towers collapsed, thick dust made it dark and hard to breathe. It was terrifying, and the confusion forced people to run anywhere and everywhere to escape. This photo was taken near the waterfront at Battery Park. I heard that boats and ferries came from all over the harbor to help. Courtesy of U.S. Coast Guard

THEN — Someone stopped the music and the heartbeat of New York City went off course...forever. Courtesy of U.S. Coast Guard

ONCE UPON A TIME — We were kings and queens in a tall graceful tower, kicked back and easy in the beauty of the sky...and then...it was gone. This is my heartbreak. Courtesy of U.S. Coast Guard

THE HEART OF NYC— A close friend who wants to remain nameless volunteered for the recovery efforts immediately after 9/11. He took photos at ground zero, where only recovery workers had access. The cleanup was overwhelming.

THROUGH THE RUBBLE — Never forget that after the buildings fell and all the dust settled, the only thing left standing was an old piece of Tower One, scarred and stained and twisted into the shape of an old rusted cross. © AP Images

WILL WE FORGET?— Messages written in chalk filled park sidewalks across the five boroughs to mark the one-year anniversary. © AP Images

NEVER SEEN THE RIGHTEOUS FORSAKEN— All 14 of my siblings got together in the fall of 2001 for a family reunion in Chicago. I was unable to travel and attend. The photo doesn't show the separation that my family has experienced over the years, but it does show what my parents always hoped for.

MY YOUNGEST LOVES — My niece Jhanel is a beautiful little girl. She is constantly smiling. Here she is at the entrance to my backyard garden. Both she and that garden gave me many hours of sunshine and peace in the spring and summer of 2002. She was 6 and my garden was 2.

NEW AND IMPROVED — This is me in 2003 and in my best form. I and others from area churches served Thanksgiving dinner to the homeless on a vacant lot in the city of Newburgh, NY. We served more than 200 people that day. It was awesome.

MY NEW PASSION—
Another picture from Thanksgiving in Newburgh. I love this area. There are many opportunities to be an extension of God's grace and love. I try to do as much as I can to be His arms extended.

MY PRIDE AND JOY—
My C280 Mercedes Benz parked in my driveway. Oh yeah, and that's Eliot at 16, thinking about getting behind the wheel of it. I lost my home, my garden, and my car about a year later.

WOMEN OF FAITH—
I love author Patsy Clairmont (on the right). She was VERY instrumental in my recovery in that I identified with her fears and anxieties. She heard my testimony and met with me and my friends at a Women of Faith Conference in 2004. I'll never forget her warm hug and sincere prayer. With me is Shannon, Diane, and Shannon's mom, Ann.

There were hundreds on board, rushing about, looking into the water, and grabbing life jackets like on a scavenger hunt . . . not frantically, and not everyone, but purposefully. I might have wondered what they knew that I didn't. I turned to speak with Nancy, but she was out of sight by then.

That's when I saw Lorna. She was visibly shaken and sitting near the side of the ferry. Her face is still as clear to me now as it was that day. She looked drained and aged. Her makeup had faded from crying and her hair was no longer perfect. She was trembling and tousled.

I stared as she described seeing the second plane fly into Tower Two. "I kept waiting for it to pull up, but . . . it just went right in."

I don't know if it was disbelief or denial, but she relived the entire thing while shaking her head back and forth, gesturing no. "I . . uh . . . it . . . there was a huge hole in the side of the building, Leslie."

I listened and was amazed to hear that there had in fact been not one but two attacks. It was the first conversation that really registered for me all day registered and delivered another devastating blow. I watched this big beautiful woman become smaller with every syllable.

It is illogical looking back, but even though we lived it, neither of us had any idea of the infamy September 11 would later claim. We were clueless that even as early as 8:50 A.M., the day had moved beyond a date on the calendar and into something bigger and of a much greater magnitude than what we could wrap our minds around . . . ever. We were just too small.

Suddenly there was a terrible sound like a freight train coming.

I SAW THIS IN A DREAM . . .

The walls were hollow and pitch-black. Nothing was solid. Everything that existed there was a mist but still able to be touched. I was there for a reason, but I didn't know why. I knew that I wasn't ready for whatever was ahead. I tried to tell the Lord no. I tried to tell Him to wait, but my mouth sealed and I could not speak. I was "me" but I was watching myself from somewhere outside of it all.

I stood motionless in darkness with my back pressed firmly against a mirrored wall that I could not see; expecting that at any moment something would devour me. My senses sharpened and I could feel the presence of something very evil. "Jesus Christ is my Lord," I screamed at the top of my voice. Nothing came from my mouth. I passed by a mirror and saw a face like mine. It approached me quickly in body only—then dissipated. My face itched and then my entire body. Terror gripped my knees and forced my hands to my eyes. "Jesus Christ is my Lord," I shouted again and again.

There was movement about me, and faces I'd never seen before, some just figures of faces with no features at all . . . just blank and empty. Though I had never seen them, I knew them. Then suddenly I was angry, so angry that my breathing quickened and my muscles tensed. My fists balled and my back released the wall. I reached inside of me, with all the strength and faith I could collect, and I shouted with authority . . . "Jesus Christ is my Lord!"

I looked back to Manhattan Island in stillness.

There it stood in the unfamiliar magnificence of surrender—WEAK.

Then, in almost perfect rhythm and easy gracefulness—in a huge cloud of black smoke—over in seconds—gone—FAILED.

Tower Two surrendered her ghosts—COLLAPSED.

"Ashes to ashes and dust to dust."

Jesus wept. (John 11:35)

CHAPTER 12

It Is Finished

There Is No Other Love

For God so loved the world that he gave his
one and only Son, that whoever believes in
him shall not perish but have eternal life.

—JOHN 3:16

The crowd that had been standing and watching the fires
found itself in the path of a slaughtered giant. No one hesitated
to move. For miles, the rumble of thunder drowned out the cries
of the city. More horrified screams and shrieks of panic rose from
the streets of Manhattan and invaded every living room in the
world. It was almost a synthesized movement as people turned
to run. They pushed the people in front of them and used each
other to propel themselves faster in a desperate attempt to
escape . . . and then, the deafening, angry thunder and the all-
consuming black cloud. . . .

I still hear it sometimes.

I MET A MAN MANY YEARS AGO who told me that He loved me. I fell in love with His majesty. I fell in love with His love for me. For me, He created the world and its entire splendor. For His praise and pleasure, His hands molded the earth and filled it with every awesome thing, great and small.

From my heart, I hear shouts of His praise.

From every view on earth, His glory reigns.

From the birds that sing in synchronicity, to winds that whistle a melody—He is a poet.

From the trees that bathe in the sun to color the mountain's landscape, to flowers that share His fragrant breath—He is an artist.

He declares the sun to shine and the moon to glow.

The oceans still and seas rumble on His word.

He breathes life with a thought and His whisper conquers death.

With the wave of His hand, He spins the earth and writes its history—He is an author.

He delivers and heals, He grieves and gives comfort, He chastens and consoles, He forgives and forgets, loves and loves, and then loves more.

He is "Our Father." My father . . . my Beloved.

Selah

I got off the ferry at the Hoboken train terminal with a pounding headache and completely absent from my body. I was dizzy, dazed, and exhausted.

Nancy and I hugged, exchanged numbers, and went our separate ways. I stood in the middle of the station for a while doing nothing, just standing. What I needed was a long nap, and had it not been for the madness in the train station, I could have easily lain down on one of the wooden benches in the waiting area and quietly passed away.

To think only a few hours before, the train station had been busy with normal commuter insolence in their hurry to "get there." Newspaper stands had been active and the smell of coffee and cigarettes prominent. Hundreds of commuters had been on their way to work with morning papers tucked neatly under their arms and their briefcases hurriedly flung over their shoulders. Each one had glanced at the clock and hurried toward the PATH trains with the same purpose of getting to work and making the day go by fast, in order to get back home.

Now, in the moment that I was living, hundreds of disheveled commuters without briefcases were desperately looking for a train out—out of the nightmare—out of the city and out of the loop!

Security was understandably tight. Police officers, PA announcements, shaken conductors, medics, and crew members told bits of the story as it came through over the radio and TV. Paranoia crept in. Were the commuter trains about to be attacked? Was it safe to ride? Is there a situation in the tunnels? Is it over? Let's beat up the Muslims in the station store. He looks like a terrorist. What is he carrying? Sir, will you step this way, please?

It was a mess. As it turned out, trains did not enter or leave the station for hours. Medics checked the injured and took blood pressure readings and we were free to go.

> Disheveled commuters without briefcases were desperately looking for a train out—out of the nightmare.

I walked back and forth for a few minutes trying to regain a sense of direction. Then, exasperated at my own dithering, I finally stood near the arrival/departure board and checked for train and track information. The schedules changed by the minute. A conductor came over to me. He had a puzzled look on his face. He looked me up and down and asked if I was okay. I nodded. "Sure." It was later that I came to understand why he asked.

On an average day, it was simply not normal to walk about wearing clothes stained with blood and dust. It wasn't an everyday thing to wander through train stations with singed facial hair and burns and bruises about the head and hands. Sadly, that day, it probably was the least of what passed through the station.

He helped me board the correct train. "Just wait here," he said. "We'll leave shortly." I nodded and boarded.

Different from my usual commuter habit, I sat next to someone, a co-worker named John. I took a deep breath. He was in tears and spouting something about the Pentagon and Camp David and Pennsylvania and this being worse than Pearl Harbor and my goodness he didn't breathe once. He was understandably livid and cussing like he was insane. He said he wanted to reenlist and find "that black-hearted [expletive] coward." I smiled politely and thought that maybe the shouting crowd had been right. Maybe this did mean war. But that thought was even scarier than what I was living through. War would kill us all.

"I saw the second plane hit," someone yelled. "I was near the window and could have been killed," someone else said. "Oh, my God, did you see the bodies?" another shouted. Everyone around me was sharing the fear, the rage, or the pain in one language or another. Some were praying. I think it would have been beautiful had it not been for the circumstances . . . the solidarity, I mean.

Everybody was anxious as the train sat idle. Everybody spent nervous energy that kept them talking about anything and everything—from revenge to solidarity to information on hijackings to peanut butter sandwiches, believe it or not.

I just sat with my hands tucked under my armpits, rocking back and forth. All the conversations around me blended. What began as audible, distinguishable sentences became nothing more than a barrage of garbled gabble.

Then came the antidote to all gibberish—a passenger who had been listening to a small radio jumped from his seat, pounded the headrest of the seat in front of him, and wailed, "Tower One just fell . . . Tower One just fell . . . Oh, my God . . . Tower One just fell. Dear God, help us! Oh, help us! Those [expletive] are blowing up New York!"

"What?" John asked. "Oh, my God . . . no!" He jumped forward in his seat and sobbed angrily. His face was beet red and he almost collapsed to the floor. The news of the second Twin's demise traveled throughout the train like weeds, almost visibly growing.

It began as a rumble and a very slow build . . . a wave of emotion . . . a rhythm . . . almost like feet softly stamping in a ballpark and working toward a climax . . . or a reverse echo . . . until finally the angst and the loathing erupted into an enormous roar and swallowed up all remaining life on that train.

It lasted. . . .

> If only for one day, the weeping, the prayers, and the hand-holding erased all barriers.

I was astounded by the commonality brought about by such extreme distress. If only for one day, the weeping, the prayers, and the hand-holding erased all barriers. We were a united people. And, if not for the obvious presence of the snake, the scene on that train could have represented a perfect world.

I turned to John. "What happened?" I asked calmly. "Our building just fell," he said. "What?" "It's down," he answered. I think I heard impatience in his voice. "Gone, Leslie . . . both towers are gone."

I guess I asked the wrong question. What I really wanted was for him to explain to me what we had just gone through. *What* happened?

What I got was a moment of clarity. As the haze in my mind began to clear, all of my whats became whys and I stared blankly out the window. It is finished.

> Men never do evil so completely and cheerfully as when they do it from religious conviction. —Pascal

I think hours passed before that train moved. I lost time.

Finally, it pulled out of Hoboken Terminal. It rounded the corner at a snail's pace, and everyone stared out the windows. Some stood in the aisles to see and some even tiptoed over seats. What we saw stopped our hearts.

There's a rhythm to life. Things move to a beat and play to inspire our journeys. From the waves in the womb to rock-a-bye baby, from the swinging arms of a mother to the motion of cars, sports, and dance—even death, sleeping, and eating have a beat. Rhythm is life.

> As the haze in my mind began to clear, all of my whats became whys.

We live by it. We expect the music. Our habits, behaviors, thoughts, and activities are melodic and keep up with the beat. When in harmony, they captivate us and inspire our life stories. We call them our songs.

Incomparable to any other addiction, source of intoxication, or "fix," every person on earth is driven by and addicted to the rhythms of life. Skip a beat, miss the melody, lose step, or stop the music, even for a minute, and the heart can go off course forever.

We rounded that curve, leaving New York City, where it was all about the rhythm of the Big Apple skyline, and someone stopped the music. There it was. Amidst billowing clouds of smoke, beneath an ocean of uncollected tears and countless personal items, the new and not-so-improved New York skyline . . . with no towers. Both were gone.

I believe every eye on the train filled with tears and incredulity. Although the rhythm was enough to keep the momentum, it was not enough to define the music, and the heart of all of New York City went off course . . . forever.

PART THREE

Miles to Go Before I Sleep

CHAPTER 13

Going Home

No Words

Let us search and try our ways, and turn
again to the Lord.

—LAMENTATIONS 3:40 KJV

A WEALTHY MAN HAD TWO SONS. *The younger son asked his father for his inheritance. Shortly after receiving it, the son gathered his things and left for a "far country." He spent his money on fancy living, enjoying parties, expensive clothes, drugs, and anything that made him feel good. He thought he was living "the good life." During this time, he forgot about God.*

Soon his money ran out and hard times hit the country. He had no money for food or clothing, so he went to work for a man who sent him into the fields to feed his pigs. By then he was so hungry that he wanted to eat the pigs' food. He found himself on his hands and knees, humiliated. In extreme anxiety, he remembered that even the servants in his father's house had more than enough to eat and were well cared for.

"I will go back to my father, and I will say to him, 'Father, I have sinned against heaven and you.' " He got up from his place of disgrace and started home to his father's house.

I rode the train in complete silence. I didn't want to open my mouth. I didn't want to see, taste, hear, or know anything else . . . ever. I kept fidgeting and trying not to think about what had just happened. I wanted not to think about friends that I had left behind.

Everyone on the train was reaching out to their loved ones, using cell phones and writing e-mails. There we were, survivors, reeling from the shock of our morning; many aware of our need for God but still not calling to Him. Instead, we used our cell phones to call our homes. It's a perfectly natural right . . . to reach out to our loved ones in times of stress.

Eventually I tried calling Eliot's school and then his grandmother. It was difficult recalling phone numbers, and when I did, I couldn't get a signal. After trying a few times, I gave up and leaned back to relax, but I couldn't fight back thoughts about what had happened. *Was it really an act of terrorism? Why would they attack us? What were they planning? Were they now attacking upstate, burning down schools and wreaking havoc near my home?* I started fidgeting again and looking in my laptop bag . . . for nothing.

John squirmed too. He peered out the windows and babbled to himself from time to time about reenlisting and Pearl Harbor. His anger took control of him. His face became red and he squeezed his fists tighter and tighter when he spoke. I saw his teeth clenched behind his jaws in a nervous mania between action and resolute anger. I was afraid for him. I was afraid of him. I was scared that somehow our government, now faced with war, was so angry, desperate, and afraid that it would allow John and all the "Johns" in the U.S. to go fight.

"Please, John, try to relax. Okay?" He looked at me as if I had said the most absurd thing he had ever heard. I closed my eyes. I wanted to ignore him and the gigantic headache that was splitting my head into pieces.

The train rattled along in silence. The conductor didn't even announce the stops.

We arrived at John's stop. Mine was next. He looked at me almost questioningly and said, "Take care, Leslie." I nodded and we hugged good-bye. My heart skipped a beat. I was afraid, nervous, and didn't want to be alone. *What if something bad happened on the train?* I was afraid even to go home.

> *What if something bad happened on the train? I was afraid even to go home.*

GOD GAVE ME MY DAUGHTER IN 2000. *Monai came to live with me when she was sixteen. In my eyes she was a shy and still angry little girl who doubted her worthiness to be loved. She was unsure about life and confused about me.*

She didn't remember her biological mother and couldn't understand how a mom could walk away from her child. I watched her get lost searching for meaning in her memories and withdraw. I watched her sometimes move from laughter to anger in minutes. As difficult as it was at times, I made a commitment and I loved her.

I looked for ways to convince her to trust me. Though it wasn't easy, after almost a year of finding the balance between long lectures and longer hugs, lots of questions and more answers, I saw the emergence of a beautifully confident young woman. There was light growing inside those dark eyes and I loved it.

Though legally Monai is still not mine, our matters are now heart matters, and so she calls me her Leslie and lets me call her my daughter. She has embraced the family tradition of Friday nights and pizza, and with the exception of Eliot, she is the only person I know who can watch the same movie three times in one night . . . blissfully.

I felt panic grow inside me when I realized how scared and lonely Monai must have been feeling. She wouldn't survive losing another mother. "Dear God, take care of my family. Please let my children be all right. Keep them safe and comfort them."

My stop.

I got off the train and walked toward my car. The air was still thin and crisp—fresh and undaunted by the events in Manhattan. I was miles away and safe. . . .

The walk through the parking lot was strange. I was hypersensitive. I kept noticing my feet. I could feel every muscle and nerve ending in my soles as they struck the hard cement beneath them.

My skin was so sensitive and my senses were overly aware of everything. I even noticed a subtle shift in the wind.

It was a primal, almost instinctive awareness that made me even more panicky at the sounds of hustling feet and starting cars. I looked around nervously at a few other passengers moving at a fast pace toward their cars. The sound of my own quick breaths startled me. I could hear myself breathe from deep within my chest again. It echoed.

As I approached the center of the parking lot, which by now was almost empty, my heart beat faster. I had parked in the same place I always did, so I walked toward my car with no clear or cognizant thoughts. Getting home would be the challenge. *Okay, okay,* I thought. *Which way is home?* I started my car and drove. I don't know how fast or how slow, I just drove—feeling the air in my face and inhaling the crisp air that lingered around the mountains. I almost closed my eyes. If I had any presence of mind at all, I would have been wishing that I had stretched that morning's seventeen-minute drive to twenty-five, at a cruising speed of thirty miles per hour, to miss the morning train and have that hooky day.

The second is this: "Love your neighbor as yourself." There is no commandment greater than these. (Mark 12:31)

I MOVED INTO MY HOME in March of 1997. I spent the first weekend cleaning, polishing, and congratulating myself on my accomplishment. By the third day, my neighbors Marcia Kissel and her daughter Valerie surprised me with a large plate of homemade coconut cookies and a "welcome to the neighborhood" card. It was love at first sight, with the cookies. Marcia took some getting used to.

About sixty-five years old, Marcia is full of sincerity, love, and words of wisdom. She has a quiet unassuming presence, but is very deliberate in her actions. Her fine blond hair has soft shades of gray throughout. She wears it neatly combed and pulled back from her round, beautifully aged face. With a slow, intentional grace and ease of civility, Marcia offers advice to every open, or not, ear.

Not even a month after I had moved in, she was excusing herself and telling me what not to do in my flower garden, and watching my son play in the backyard or swim in the pool. There she was offering a keen eye, a phone call, or just words of wisdom. I thought to myself, Oh, boy, another mother.

September 11, 2001
Time Unknown

I pulled into my driveway and saw Marcia standing in her driveway talking with Valerie. I calmly got out of the car and lifted my hand to wave hello, but "hello" never happened.

What did happen however, was "that" scream. The scream that had started deep in my belly hours before and growled in my gut every time I saw a body or body part; the scream that got bigger every time I passed another person too afraid to escape and paralyzed me each time I ignored a cry for help. The scream that had haunted me in the stairs, on the concourse, and through the halls. The scream that had stolen my breath and left me spent and hopeless time after time. The scream that had waited idle until now.

I felt it reach down deep in my gut, gather to itself every emotion that I had experienced all day, expand beyond my own understanding, and consume every inch of available space outside of me. It robbed me of my knees, stole any remaining sense of place, time, and self, and . . .
EXPLODED!

I WAILED!

> I calmly got out of the car and lifted my hand to wave hello, but "hello" never happened.

Marcia would have to describe what exactly happened next as I only remember seeing her jump the fence between our homes. I remember a bath, the feel of the water washing away dust and smoke and tears and blood and visions and pain and years of ego, pride, and self-righteousness. I remember the safety of Marcia's lap and her warm soft hands stroking my face and quietly whispering to me.

There is something very special about true love. Unfortunately, many of us only recognize it in retrospect.

Thank God for advice about flowers and for neighbors who care enough to watch your children play safely and offer kind words of wisdom. Thank God for *another* mother.

After my bath, I turned the television on to the news. Marcia strongly advised against it, but I had to see it for myself. I needed answers.

Every station played clips of the attack. Newscasters themselves were emotionally tossed and struggled to put the pieces together.

They stumbled over words like "This just in" and "In an apparent terrorist attack" while a traumatized world watched the towers collapse over and over again. How could they convey to a revenge-hungry, even ravenous country, a carnage that they themselves did not understand?

The whole world was in shock, and the media struggled to recapture that one moment at 8:46 A.M. that changed the course of our nation.

I will never forget the confusion I felt when I saw the TV coverage for the first time. Had it not been for the fact that I was there when it happened, I would have sworn what I was seeing on the news was a different building entirely.

You see, my recollection was of a building defeated on the first blow and crumbling from the moment of impact. There was no pretense on the inside. Beams were contracting, walls were caving in, and floors collapsed seconds after the first impact. That building was coming down.

What I experienced was not a conspiracy or question of how many bombs went off and caused the fall. It was quite honestly a towering inferno, and its demise was like 110 stories of dominos, the first one tipped when an American Airlines weapon of mass destruction crashed into Tower One.

Every channel showed what they thought they saw, which was two towers after the initial attack with some damage from the crashes and a lot of smoke. What cameras saw from the outside was NOT what was going on inside. They showed the world the towers severely injured but standing strong and still fighting.

It is no wonder the world was surprised when they fell. It is no wonder that the shock wave was so all-consuming that it left our president speechless. They never saw it coming.

Marcia spoke later about times changing and sleeper cells, and then President Bush gave foreign nations an immediate choice in their relationship with the United States. In plain English, black and white, he said, "You're either with us or you're against us" in the fight against terrorism.

These were powerful words, and at first everyone applauded his boldness. The words *good* and *evil* incited ideas of "justice" and restored our belief in "freedom." The notion of a war on terror and obliterating Osama bin Laden and al-Qaeda were quickly embraced. What we were blinded to in our demand for justice was that a war on terror meant more people would die.

My phone rang.

"Hello."

"Leslie?"

"Yes. Lawrence?"

"Yes. Are you okay, little girl?"

"I think so." Silence. Then the question, "Lawrence, does this mean what I think it means?"

With no hesitation came the answer, "Yes."

I cried. He told me he would pray for me, and we hung up the phone.

My brother has always been my rod. I weigh the significance of most things by his reactions or his words. Neither of us needed full sentences to understand the other. Now he was confirming for me that 8:46 that morning did not simply mark the beginning of a war or change the course of our nation; it was much more significant than just that. It signaled the crossing over of time in the end of days.

My attention turned back to the TV coverage, almost expecting to see Jesus in the clouds. I'm not sure if I was more terrified of

Osama bin Laden or Jesus Christ's return. In that moment, neither looked good to me. I wasn't ready.

> I'm not sure if I was more terrified of Osama bin Laden or Jesus Christ's return.

I was so shook up that I passed out on Marcia's lap. She held me.

I woke to a surreal type of silence, then a screech of tires in my driveway. I peed on myself. Monai walked through the door slowly at first, cautiously and unsure. She was obviously dreading what she might find in place of the woman she watched leave for work that morning. She looked at me but kept her distance. Her eyes filled. The sigh from her heart filled the room.

Then, just behind her, my joy returned to me. I opened wide my arms to receive my only son. He ran to me with tears of relief and praises to the Lord for bringing Mommy home. I exhaled his name . . . Eliot.

We looked at each other and cried tears of joy in the unfamiliar beauty of surrender—WEAK.

We merged the weight of every power lunch and play date until we could in perfect rhythm and easy gracefulness release the day—FAILED.

We embraced the new beat—COLLAPSED.

> But the father said to his servants . . . "Let's have a feast and celebrate. For this son of mine was dead and is alive again; he was lost and is found." So they began to celebrate. (Luke 15:22, 24)

I was home!

CHAPTER 14

Strike Three

Post-Traumatic Stress Disorder and Learning to Breathe

Journal Entry

October 2001

She claims she wants me to explain why I wouldn't stay in that psych ward, but I know she knows. . . . I'm not that crazy. GOD!!!!!!!!!! *Ahhhhhh!!!*

I don't know why she keeps asking the same questions . . . told her exactly what I remember happened the day after they tried to kill me . . . somebody drove me to Dr. Rohan's office. I think it was . . . Marcia . . . his assistant was waiting for me outside . . . she grabbed my arm and helped me in. . . . Doctor Rohan took my blood pressure . . . he made a sound like he was dying . . . p.s. everything sounds like it's dying . . . whatever the shot was, made my head hurt worse . . . he explained PTSD, gave me more pills and blah . . . what don't she understand . . . that's all I remember. Period . . . its like I'm still in that fog . . . it still feels like I'm watching it happen . . . God, please . . . please. . . .

If she thinks I'm going back to that hospital, she's got another thing comin'. . . . p.s. Ronnie left yesterday . . . again.

T his is my story. I woke up one morning, dressed in business attire, and went to work fully expecting a normal day. Instead, I rode an elevator thirty-six floors and got off in the middle of a lunatic's delusion of justice.

The terrorist attacks of September 11 shattered my life and left me with nothing to rebuild. After years of making carefully planned career decisions, fourteen-hour workdays, hundreds of power suits and power lunches, I couldn't even decide whether to get out of bed or not.

I had flashbacks that caused me to react. They felt as real as being there all over again. I could smell the building. I could hear the bells. I was drawn to roadkill. And no matter where I was when a flash-back occurred, my muscles tensed until I was in pain, and my only urge was to make it stop, even if that meant aimlessly running or doing even more unreasonable things like making my friends pull over on high mountain roads.

There were days when I had to sit down in order to feel my legs beneath me, and disturbing uncontrollable trembling forced me behind doors.

I was anxious all the time and afraid of my own backyard, convinced that the Taliban was hiding in my shed. I boarded my windows with thick wooden shutters in fear that "they" would get in and murder us all. I put homemade weapons near my bed "just in case" and prayed all night for deliverance.

My future was hopeless. Unable to cross bridges, pass through tunnels, get on elevators, or enter high-rises, I couldn't return to work. I couldn't drive without thinking that trucks alongside me were carrying missiles that would suddenly explode as I passed. I had panic attacks when left alone and anxiety attacks when too many people were around. Sleep was impossible without sleeping pills, which only worked for a few hours.

I would lie awake and watch the sky in fear of what might fall. I walked the floors, jumped at every unfamiliar sound, and feared that sleep would never again be something to long for. There was no end to the constant replays and haunting sounds of what I had lived through.

What was it like? Don't try to imagine that every step you take could be your last. Rather, feel your heart beating your body into an uncontrollable convulsion. What did it look like? The gruesome, the shocking, the reality is that hell must be close. How did it feel?

I was anxious all the time and afraid of my own backyard, convinced that the Taliban was hiding in my shed.

Don't feel. Rather, find yourself in a state of nothingness between a quiet slumber and a ghastly actuality—a "fog" if you will, a nightmare from which you cannot awake.

SLEEP OR SLUMBER IN a tomb of despair
The eyes of danger watching there
What price to pay or penalty to keep
For those once calming words . . . "Now I lay me down to
sleep"
Whisper to me . . . or sing me a lullaby
Of winds and of angels and of worlds that don't die
Tell me your secrets, then whisk me away
From the place of disdain in which I now lay
Ever cold, ever deep, ever-hallowed ground . . .
Sleeping here and slumbering there
Forever now—in a tomb of despair.

P TSD is probably one of the most difficult disorders to describe. It's a very mean disease. It has no friends and makes no excuses. In fact, I don't believe a word exists in the English language that encompasses its whole sphere of related emotions, symptoms, and overall feeling of being "finished."

In the months following the tragedy, reality was still too big for me to wrap my arms around it all. I couldn't face the details, so I withdrew from therapy. I went to the sessions, but that's all.

Doctors suggested it would be years before I would be able to process everything and regain full mental capacity. They even considered the possibility that I might never return to a truly "productive" state of mind.

Days went by before I could leave my home. Weeks passed and I had yet to fully realize the enormity of rubble replacing my towers. I saw more than a fair share of mindless days spent doing absolutely nothing but wishing my misery away.

Months passed before I slept. Years have gone by and some details are still lost. Every now and then old colleagues feed me bits and pieces of what might be buried inside me.

Some have suggested that it was in fact the street-level of the concourse where I was lost and not the plaza. Others remember seeing me picking up body parts rather than stepping over them. Marcia, my neighbor, spoke about me taking a shower and asking for cigarettes, and by the way, she was sixty-one.

Although I have accepted the fact that some details are probably forever lost in the catacombs and grand ruins of what was once my future, I still listen to my friends with an almost unbearable desire to put their pieces together with mine and finally see the big picture.

I have struggled, and as upsetting a reality as it might be, I have considered all of the what–ifs. I realize that one pause too many or one step in the wrong direction could have been fatal. What if the airplane had hit the tower lower or just fifteen minutes earlier; if I had left the stairs as the stranger suggested; if the last door had never opened. My story would be one of the unknown. Instead, this is my testimony of God's grace.

Journal Entry

I dreamed I was at work, but this time I was carrying a rope. The plane hit the tower as it had before, but instead of going into shock, I walked through the entire building blowing a horn and telling people to leave. This time I threw a rope from the 99th floor all the way to the ground so that people could slide down to the crowd on the streets. One by one, they went before me and I coordinated the entire thing. I never saw the end of the dream. I woke up in distress, sweating, hyperventilating in a panic and in tears.

Journal Entry

I went into the basement again today. This time I stayed down there longer. I walked all the way to the other side holding my breath and trying to imagine what it's like being buried alive. I closed my eyes, but never got past being alone. I can't imagine what Michael went through. I never got past being alone.

Journal Entry

Ronnie's gonna try to leave again tomorrow. He has to get back to school. I'm so scared I don't know what to do. I can't bear the thought of being alone. Who's gonna protect me and Eliot? Oh God, please help me!!!!!!!!!

I survived the attack, yes, but there is nothing particularly special about me. I am an everyday kind of woman. The woman you see sitting alone on the park bench—pensive. The one awkwardly smiling as she squeezes into the pew next to you on Sunday morning—late. I am that woman counting in her head and fidgeting with her groceries at checkout—average, normal, everyday. And in my everyday is where God collected all my symptoms and I began to live again.

Pastor John Torres is a lot like my brother Lawrence. He is a very private, calm man with a very deliberate way about him. He doesn't waste words. He says what he means and means what he says in a kind but firm sort of way.

One day, almost a year after the attacks, I sat in his office confused, looking for answers and trying to figure out how to tell him that most nights I still lie awake wanting to tear through my own skin to escape the pain. I spoke softly, stammering, trying to process through the trauma by giving him a minute-by-minute account of what had happened.

He listened for almost an hour, and then interrupted. "You know, Leslie," he said. "It's okay to move slowly through your journey to healing. It's okay to still be disturbed by what you remember and it's even okay not to be okay. God's grace is never ending. His mercies go on for as long as you need them . . . forever."

God's grace and His mercies endure. . . .

And so, I survived, yes, but there is no self-righteousness with me, no delusions of great spiritual discernment. I'm not special, nor do I know the secrets of healing through PTSD beyond what has been revealed through modern medicine.

What I know is that God's grace really is so much more than sufficient and His mercy covers multitudes of pain, providing healing permanence.

And the peace of God . . .

I loved my garden. I enjoyed the texture and natural beauty of flowers and the light fragrance of spring. I'd sit in the middle of my flower beds sometimes and bury my hands in the dirt until I was euphoric. Every year I planted several varieties of flowers. Sometimes I would plant, prune, or weed until the sun went down.

One day I was pruning my roses. I handled them tenderly and with care—to make them beautiful. A thought came to my mind about how God prunes us with the same technique. I smiled at the thought of having Him touch me in any way at all. In fact, I yearned for it.

Then a plane flew overhead. I stopped breathing. Without thinking, I got up and ran down my driveway in a panic . . . going nowhere. I just reacted . . . and ran.

Miraculously, I'm past that now. I stopped running from death and found life in Jesus Christ. I found peace in believing His promise that one day after all is over, I will meet Him in a glorious celebration of overcoming. It's what I live for.

I still wake from time to time to the sickening sound of my own screams. I still grieve the loss of life and for the loved ones left behind. I still pray for the orphaned children and hope for their futures.

As shocking as it might sound, my senses still retain a bit of that day, as my sense of smell is heightened and I will walk aimlessly about a room just to find the remains of a single burned match.

I still find myself watching airplanes fly overhead. I hate the sound of their engines flying low. I don't like fire, loud and sudden noises startle me, and fireworks can bring me to tears.

But these things no longer limit my life. My days are filled to capacity with the hope of His glory. And when I feel crisp, subtle winds blowing gently across the night, and the dew tickles my skin with a playful tease—when I see the nearest cloud is a trillion light years away and stars are floating in the sky like diamonds—I smile back at God and I . . . breathe.

CHAPTER 15

The Awakening

Redemption

For I know the thoughts that I think toward you, says the Lord, thoughts of peace and not of evil, to give you a future and a hope.
—JEREMIAH 29:11 NKJV

Legend suggests that the emperor Napoleon Bonaparte referred to China as a sleeping giant. He supposedly pointed his finger at the country and remarked, "If he wakes, he will shake the world."

I grew up in a large Christian family. My parents were devout, dutiful, outspoken in their beliefs, and steadfast in their commitment to "training up" their children in the way that we should go. In doing so, they believed and followed the Word of God in its entirety, not just the easy parts.

Consequently, my brothers, sisters, and I were encouraged in our walk of faith. We were raised to know Jesus Christ first as Lord and Master, and then to know Him in much the same way that we knew each other, intimately.

As a young girl, I embraced this way of life with enthusiasm. I knew of nothing else. I was in my teenage years before I got the "taste" in my mouth. As I became more familiar with the allure of life outside my home, I wanted less of the humble and pious living taught inside it.

Looking back, I understand now that life can be enticing in its notion of success—offering its big-eyed homes and fancy cars, its big apples, bright lights, and many indulgences. For these things, I left Chicago behind.

Meanwhile, my brothers and sisters remained faithful. They stayed close to home and went about the business of living, alert and daily offering up their lives to the Lord. Gladly they conformed to His image, to be like Him; first to His beauty: pure, clean, and holy—and then to His example: faithful and true.

> My life was all about me. It was my perspective, my plans, my thoughts, and my beliefs.

Me, I served another. Bearing no resemblance at all to the girl of my youth, I became arrogant, cold, and aloof. My life was all about me. It was my perspective, my plans, my thoughts, and my beliefs. I was the center of my own world. I existed for the pleasures built by my own hands, within the small and feeble self-constructed fences of my own will; I was an odyssey unto me. Egotistical and materialistic, I sought every "thing" that didn't matter. In exchange for all the glitter of this world's "something owned," I knowingly packed away the Love of my youth and ignored Him.

As time passed, it became easier and easier to rationalize my sin.

I reasoned that even though I was no longer following Christ, I was still a good person because I was moral. I wasn't a murderer. I only told harmless little lies. I wasn't adulterous, and fornication, after all, was just old-fashioned ideology. I wasn't a thief and I didn't actually love money; it was merely a means to an end—building a life that my children and I deserved.

I faced every day with little to no regard for the condition of my heart or God's will for my life. I was, in other words . . . oblivious. Over time, I evolved into the thing I was on that September morning.

> When I consider the short duration of my life, swallowed up in the eternity of before and after, the little space I fill, and even see, engulfed in the infinite immensity of space of which I am ignorant, and which knows me not, I am frightened and am astonished at being here rather than there. Why now rather than then. —Pascal

And so the story goes. . . .

Somehow, and despite my lack of honor, my loving Father, the Emperor of all emperors, was determined to not leave me sleeping . . . or in His words, ignorant. He waited patiently with a plan of redemption.

Looking back, I am amazed at how God works things together for His good. I am amazed at how I came to be in New York City, after traveling more than seven hundred miles from my hometown of Chicago and years of corporate climbing to work in the World Trade Center, where at 8:46 A.M. on Tuesday, September 11, 2001, I was exactly where I needed to be in order that grace might find me . . . stirring. It leaves me speechless, how He looked beyond my faults.

Grace. There I was, broken and lost among tower rubble and sin. Grace. There I was, covered in guilt and alone. Grace. There they were . . . extended . . . the loving hands of a Father rescuing His wayward little girl, in spite of herself.

My eyes fill with tears even now and my spirit leaps for joy because that is the miracle of this story. That is the love in it. That, my friend, is His amazing grace that covers my unworthiness and then covers me. It is the undeserved favor of a loving Father toward His child.

God's grace has nothing to do with any goodness of ours, who we are, what we know, or where we are in life. It has all to do with the nature of Him. What a beautiful revelation. What a beautiful truth!

Months after 9/11, after throwing away meds, surrendering my symptoms to the Lord, and acknowledging my need for Him, I gave my whole self to the Lord. My brother Lawrence celebrated with me. In a later conversation, he said he didn't believe that the Lord would have had him pray for me for so long if God hadn't intended to save me. Lawrence then asked me to talk about my commitment to the Lord and what had changed in me since that terrible day.

It took almost three years before I could answer him with confidence. Three years to qualify what I had been through, understand the emotions and theology of it all, and then finally find words that expressed my whole heart.

How long wilt thou forget me, O Lord? for ever?
How long wilt thou hide thy face from me?
How long shall I take counsel in my soul,

having sorrow in my heart daily?

How long shall mine enemy be exalted over me?

Consider and hear me, O Lord my God:

lighten mine eyes, lest I sleep the sleep of death;

lest mine enemy say, I have prevailed against him;

and those that trouble me rejoice when I am moved.

But I have trusted in thy mercy;

my heart shall rejoice in thy salvation.

I will sing unto the Lord,

because he hath dealt bountifully with me.

—Psalm 13:1–6 KJV

September 11, 2001, became a cornerstone in my life. After building so much of nothing, all the material things I valued came down with the towers. Not at the hands of terrorists, but at the word of a carpenter, Jesus.

I lost everything. There was no substantial 9/11 victims' compensation given to me, no safety net waiting in the winds. My car was repossessed. My accounts were past due and overdrawn, and eventually, most of my friends grew tired of my asking for help and stopped answering my calls. Eliot and I suffered immensely, until finally, with what seemed to be the whole world watching, I lost my home. It was unreal. My son and I were homeless.

I often wonder where God's arms stop reaching when we fold our own. . . .

WHEN ELIOT WAS IN FIRST GRADE, *he had a nightmare that woke him. I jumped out of bed and ran to his room, only to find him hiding under the covers and crying. Gently I pulled the blanket back and asked him what was wrong. He looked at me with those big brown eyes and explained his dream. He thought someone was going to steal him away. I smiled, stroked his face, and told him a story about being a prince in Africa. I told him that at night angels came to his room while he slept, to protect him and watch over him. I told him that as they watch through the night, they play with his toys.*

For months after that, I would sneak into his room while he was sleeping, shift his toys, and pose his action figures. One night I fell asleep without shifting them. I woke the next morning to a deliriously happy little boy pointing at newly posed action figures.

As the last of our things were loaded onto the moving truck, I watched as Eliot struggled to explain to his friend why we were leaving our home. He was choked up but trying to keep his composure for my sake.

My eyes saw the pain on his face as we drove away from home . . . for the last time. My mind saw that little boy hiding under the covers and crying, expecting Mom to make him safe. My mouth opened for words to console him, but this time I had no stories to tell.

There are few things more painful in my world than seeing my son suffer and being unable to help, but I don't know if I could be who I am today without knowing such pain or suffering such great loss.

Still, there are certain implications of being on such a journey and expectations are great. After having survived and after being "brought back" from insanity, there are those who want to give my life more importance. It seems that I should have some serious words of wisdom to share. Perhaps these pages should contain some great original thought or an epiphany that explains it all and then saves the world.

Even more so, after what I witnessed in spirit, there should be an aura of God's anointing following me around, playing music above my head and whispering the secrets of the universe to me nonstop. Perhaps I should have great faith and now be able to stand unwavering through life's storms.

If only that were true.

I am weedy. I still cringe at sudden winds and brace myself to be "hewn down" at harvest time. My inspiration comes by way of these storms, and as I move through them, my eyes climb high above the soils of despair. There is "an awakening."

> God allowed me to choose my life and then He molded the consequences of those choices to bring me closer to Him.

Why the change? To what do I attribute this miracle? I don't believe in luck. Nor do I ascribe to the school of thought that suggests an indiscriminate chain of events guides us to random and inconsequential points in time. Life is more meaningful than that. It has much greater impact.

I believe that God allowed me to choose my life and then He molded the consequences of those choices to bring me closer to Him. I chose a path that led me to the World Trade Center. He chose the road that led me out. God knew all that it would take to bring me to my knees before Him . . . in repentance AND in love. He knew exactly what would send me running into His open arms, and it did.

I can't say precisely what things in life will lead you into His arms. Nor can I suggest the exact path of redemption for every person.

I suggest to you that sometimes a quiet voice wakes us, and sometimes it takes suffering. Sometimes tragedy of unparalleled proportions will turn our faces toward God and sometimes a simple song will do it. Sometimes only the enormity of falling giants can shrink our ever-growing egos enough to wake us that we might shake the world . . . for Him.

> If anyone is in Christ, he is a new creation; old things have passed away; behold, all things have become new. (2 Corinthians 5:17 NKJV)

So, my dear friend, how have I changed?

My obsession with corporate gain was replaced by a commitment to a life of service. Ministry to women and children who are homeless and victims of domestic violence suits me much better than Armani. I much prefer serving up meals on urban street corners and hot dogs from the trunk of my car to being served at a power lunch in a Wall Street restaurant.

I am steadfast now, committed to providing whatever service I can in order to be the outstretched arms of Jesus Christ. Not for my glory, but for His alone. I serve better when I am humbled, and I teach best what I need most to learn. Only God gives a life fulfilled.

By God's grace, Eliot and I made it through more than three years of financial struggles and four months of being homeless. We embrace our pain and loss. We have learned to direct our eyes up toward heaven. These times shape our truth, our soul, our lives, and our journey.

So now, finally I can answer what has changed in me:

Perhaps a songwriter said it simplest and said it best. "Amazing grace, how sweet the sound that saved a wretch like me. I once was lost but now am found, was blind but now I see."

Finally, through all the noise of construction . . . I . . . am . . . awake.

Selah.

CHAPTER 16

Light of the World

Into the Heart of Islam

O Lord,
Remember not only the men and women of
good will, but also those of ill will. But do
not remember all of the suffering they have
inflicted upon us: Instead remember the fruits
we have borne because of this suffering, our
fellowship, our loyalty to one another, our
humility, our courage, our generosity, the
greatness of heart that has grown from this
trouble. When our persecutors come to be
judged by you, let all of these fruits that we
have borne be their forgiveness.

—FOUND IN THE CLOTHING OF A DEAD
CHILD AT RAVENSBRÜCK
CONCENTRATION CAMP

I woke to a familiar scene.

It was more than a beautiful morning. The sun was already beginning to show her face and the sky was a brilliant blue. The kind of blue you see in island waters that once glanced, imprints itself a lasting image. Birds were singing and the wind was calm and gentle with the scent of fresh flowers and cleanly cut grass. The air was stimulating. Everything was alive! It was the kind of day that inspired being in love and the appreciation of love. It was a day that brought beauty to perfection.

I was out of bed and dressed by six A.M. with my portable CD player attached to my waist and the sounds of Bebo Norman in my ear, I set off through the mountains. I loved my early morning walks. The trails were inspiring.

I could count on the sun casting its familiar, long shadows on the ground and stimulating my appreciation for being alive. The beauty of the overlook inspires worship and I am tempted by the depths of the clouds. I could live there.

Chirping birds make me smile, and if I could somehow get butterflies to land on my hand, I would be in paradise.

Now then . . . the sound of rubber and gravel under my feet and the pace of my own heart echo around my head, while the barely audible murmur of my own singing makes my passion for the Lord . . . physical.

I had walked these trails hundreds of times before, singing and talking to the Lord. But this morning is different. This morning I am listening. This morning, through the open heart of a CD, there is an insistent yet gentle call.

Forgiveness is absolute.

These are the moments of true spiritual insight in my life. They come when I am alone and open up my heart.

I was completely absorbed into the picturesque beauty of the mountains surrounding me. My pace quickened, and as I looked out over the fields through the shadows, the fresh smell of dew-covered grass, combined with the damp, early-morning summer chill, brought about a flood of memories.

Mike. Steve. Linda . . . and that scream.

Just then, the air took my attention away; nothing quite as wholesome as crisp morning dew, almost violet. I wanted to bathe in it. Escape.

These are moments of a hushed rhythm. They are sweet moments of quiet openness, when I feel raw, hungry, and for a split second, consumed by that moment. I feel the air under my skin. I smell the end of summer with my whole body. These moments are charged. They are the ones that get me, way down deep in my soul.

Forgiveness is intended.

"Great Light of the World" played in my ear and I was aware of God's presence. The lyrics spoke loud into my heart. Bebo is asking God to fill up his soul with the light of His grace.

It became my prayer. His Spirit enveloped me and I cried. He wrapped around me like a warm blanket and then poured Himself all over me. I inhaled His name, *Sweet Jesus. I am so in love with this man!*

We were now at a place where I could hear Him speak to me of forgiveness; on my knees and listening. My whole self tingled.

Have you ever been in the presence of God . . . so close and oh . . . so . . . gentle . . . that it moved you off your feet and to your knees . . . prostrate before Him . . . barefaced and kissing the dirt . . . until all you were was . . . basic?

For the first time, I cried with my whole heart and soul—with abandon—like there was no one else in the world but me, and Islam.

I fell to the ground and my knees scraped against the gravel. Tears poured down my face. I was weak and divided and I remembered . . . everything that I couldn't forget. I remembered what they did. I remembered all that they did—the massacre, the horror, and all the intent.

Then . . . I let go.

For the first time, I cried with my whole heart and soul.

You see, I knew in my heart that there was no turning back. Because when it is time to leave a place, it is impossible to stay. I was moving on.

Forgiveness is not conditional.

And be kind to one another, tenderhearted, forgiving one another, even as God in Christ forgave you. (Ephesians 4:32 NKJV)

And then, but not suddenly, through all the heartache and pain, the Lord took my hand. I followed Him into the heart of Islam, and I forgave them. Somehow, the calm of His voice and sweet, sweet aroma of His breath made it so much easier.

I finally prayed for them. I prayed that God would turn them from their ways, mend our wounds, heal our hearts, save souls, and deliver us all.

Please don't misunderstand; I still ache for my friends and miss them. I still pray for the children who lost parents and the parents who lost their children.

Sometimes I can cry at night when I consider the implications of jihad. But only for a second, because there is security in knowing that MY GOD is the one true God . . . and then I fall asleep, resting comfortably in His peace.

Forgiveness really is divine.

I am the light of the world. Whoever follows me will never walk in darkness, but will have the light of life. (John 8:12)

CHAPTER 17

The Aftershock

Still About Love

There is a God-shaped vacuum in the heart
of every man which cannot be filled by any
created thing, but only by God the Creator,
made known through Jesus.

—Pascal

Since September 12, 2001, at least all of America has delved
beneath the surface of the previous day, looking for reasons that
explain why. We've questioned our leaders, doubted our military,
and finally, I guess because the reasons are much more than political
and much too much to accept, we decided simply to escape into the
yesteryears, the nostalgic TV Land and grandma's homemade cookies. We have taken that stroll down memory lane in hopes of recap-
turing the times when life was simpler . . . slower, and innocent.

We have relived the stories about long walks to school through
the snow and milk being delivered right to the front door. As a child,
I remember hearing all too often not to cry over spilled milk, seeing

Perry Mason before bedtime, and listening to the Motown sound that my older siblings played on our family record player.

But life today is not what it once was.

Once upon a time, in the year 2000, we were kings and queens in two tall graceful towers, kicked back and easy in the beauty of the sky. Prestige and power were plentiful in our kingdom. We were above it all in our land of abundance and pride. But then, as pride comes before a fall, and with force equal in boldness to its beginnings, our kingdom fell.

Gone are the days of nickel bread and free ice cream. Lost is the innocence of a simple stroll down a moonlit street. Forgotten are the neighborly smiles and welcoming cookies that warmed so many new homes. Welcome to the new age—where gunpowder and medicinal astringents have replaced the smell of chalkboards and pencils, and recess bells are sirens.

Welcome to the new fields of deliberation—where our innocents are exploited and our rights to defend them are challenged. This is our world today, where God's name is offensive and Wednesday night prayer meetings are the least attended church service of the week.

> Where do we go from here? How do we rebuild when we have lost so much of who we are?

Where do we go from here? How do we rebuild when we have lost so much of who we are?

How, my friends, can we attribute this change to the events of September 11 and punish that crime when we've yet to identify the one responsible? What lessons do we then learn amongst the scattered remains of human life and families ripped from the security of planned futures and thrown into an abyss of terror and ambiguity? Life has changed in more ways than what is apparent. So then, shall we hang our flags or should we count our children tonight before we sleep? What do you think, bin Laden? Should we even bother to turn on our alarms, check our windows, or lock our doors? What is the verdict, dear old Uncle Sam? Who is the enemy? Is it us? Them? And who are they that we have not seen them behind the veil? And if we do, what can we find to dwell on, amidst ghostlike faces running for their lives, long enough to spark insight?

> In faith there is enough light for those who want to believe and enough shadows to blind those who don't. —Pascal

There are many who still prefer a comfortable lie to the painful truth, so to share insight or carve up some profound wisdom would be futile. For what is wisdom, if not the ability to take truth in life experiences and translate it into life lessons?

Truth is, the ripples of thought and subsequent actions that stem from this tragedy range from quiet, subtle ones to angry, explosive ones.

For those who are willing to see, it has forced us up close, personal, and face-to-face with our own faults as human beings. We now realize that there is nothing pure about evil, and among the ruins of what was lost, the deeds of an evil man still breathes despair into our lives and this nightmare never ends.

Indeed, these acts of terror were evil, even as a gunman who spills innocent blood, a thief who takes away the purity of a child, or a drunken driver who steals away someone's future. We can no

Ah! So where do we begin when talking about that sinful nature or our relationship with God? How do we take a good and long introspective look at ourselves both corporately and individually, without making excuses, rationalizing, or pointing fingers?

There's the rub.

How do we acknowledge our need for God without first confessing the darkness of our hearts, our propensity for sin, and that we . . . man . . . from the garden seem to prefer the antithesis of peace: masterfully maneuvered schemes to conquer one another and then to burn.

I do not consider myself an expert on the heart or the nature of man. In fact, I find myself always leaning heavily on God's grace and wondering about my own responses to life. I have found, however, that for me, understanding who we are and our spiritual history makes the question of "how did this happen" with regard to September 11 a little easier to answer.

I have found that ours is a history throughout which man, being true to the nature of what the Bible calls "the old man," has mistaken fear for motivation, hatred for poetry, and vengeance for justice. We've answered to the lower calling of self-importance, and our determination for self-destruction shines on our faces like neon signs over cheap motels.

We have consistently looked past a just God, looking for trouble and finding it everywhere. Our carnal lusts have created the unimaginable, the incomprehensible, and what seems to us to be the unforgivable.

OKLAHOMA CITY—Two men were charged with bombing

the federal building in Oklahoma City on April 19, 1995. That bombing killed 169 men, women, and children, and *was*, at the time, the worst terrorist attack on American soil.

JONESTOWN—The murder/suicide of over nine hundred people in 1978 sent shockwaves throughout the world. The followers of Jim Jones, including more than 270 children, perished in a remote Guyana jungle after obeying his orders to drink cyanide-laced punch.

NUREMBERG—More than fifty years ago at the Nuremberg Trials, U.S. Supreme Court Justice Robert Jackson talked about the holocaust and the systematic murder of millions of Jews: "The crimes which we seek to condemn and punish have been so calculated, so malignant and so devastating, that civilization cannot tolerate their being ignored, because it cannot survive their being repeated."

Jackson's words apply still, they speak to a growing list of crimes that shed innocent blood, and a history saturated with it, still pregnant with secret transgressions too reprehensible to confess. They speak of a wicked nature and a nurtured evil that manifests a lust for power and control and hatred and, yes, even blood. Justifying a self-serving will, it spews itself from the snake to the beast and then sings the redemption song. But alas, my friends, there is and never will be a redemption blood of significance . . . save Calvary.

> But God demonstrates His own love toward us, in that while we were still sinners, Christ died for us. Much more then, having now been justified by His blood, we shall be saved from wrath through Him. (Romans 5:8–9 NKJV)

In spite of ourselves, God has given freely to us what we do not deserve. The most magnificent and incomparable act of love in all of history is the offering from God. He took our sins and death upon himself on a brutal and humiliating cross.

I believe that until we accept this offering of love and choose to love God more than we hate each other, the darkness of our hearts will continue to birth more black souls seeking to quench other sinister thirsts. We will continue in the tradition of man against man and the perpetual evil that resents our freedoms enough to free us from our lives . . . again . . . under the pretext of righting religious wrongs . . . again. Those things in times past that we fear will repeat themselves will do so and deliver more terror, more often and more completely . . . again.

Armed with that knowledge, I have learned that our battle is not with flesh and blood. It never has been. Our struggle takes place within, involving the same bitterness, pride, and arrogance that caused the other "fall" in the beginning. Our war is not with an enemy who lays wait in the mountains of Afghanistan or the deserts of Iraq. It is with an eternal enemy that knows our motivations sometimes better than we do.

> Our battle is not with flesh and blood. It never has been.

It is a relentless and merciless spirit, that when allowed to, controls how we make decisions, what we believe, how we live, and ultimately, how we die. It is destructive, and it comes to enslave the soul and inspire it with the love of the world, to inflame its lusts, to incite anger, to obscure the path of righteousness, and keep us in the darkness of chaos and confusion . . . without hope.

The real struggle is with leaders of another realm, in a battle that has been ongoing since the garden, and will not end until Christ's second coming.

I am persuaded that "that battle" and "that enemy" are the true motivation behind any event of terror, and at the end of the day answers the question of how such things happen.

> To them God willed to make known what are the riches of the glory of this mystery among the Gentiles: which is Christ in you, the hope of glory. Him we preach, warning every man and teaching every man in all wisdom, that we may present every man perfect in Christ Jesus. To this end I also labor, striving according to His working which works in me mightily. (Colossians 1:27–29 NKJV)

But take heart, my friends—there is good news! There is Christ, our Redeemer, who gives us hope. Hope that brings with it a break from old habits and a new life in Christ. *Amen.*

Hope that delivers faith beyond stumbling and joy beyond sleepless nights and tearstained pillows. *Selah.*

Hope that sets its sights on heavenly places, removing the sting of death, giving peace beyond terror and peace beyond fear! Amen!

Hope of life beyond a snakebite, freedom beyond its venom and love, the unchanging, immutable, and unconditional love of Jesus Christ that wraps itself around us like a warm blanket and secures us in His promise that we might know Christ in us—our Hope of Glory. *Hallelujah to the Lamb of God!*

Jesus Christ brings hope and a blessed assurance that wherever you are in life, regardless of what tragedy might strike, in changes or trials, burdens or fears . . . there IS another side to where you are, a break in tradition, and that is where hope waits. It did for me. *Selah.*

CHAPTER 18

The Authentic Voice

Never Forget

I believe in the sun even when it is not shining. I believe in love even when I'm not feeling it. I believe in God even when he is silent.

—AUTHOR UNKNOWN

The years since 9/11 have gone by much faster than we know, and somehow what should have been a flight to new heights has landed us right back where we started. Back to business as usual; back to school, to work, to church, to the laundry, the supermarket, and the ill intentions. The life of the American dream—of hot dogs, apple pie, and baseball—has resumed.

We have returned to the gyms, the parks, the playgrounds, the airplanes, the buses, our expensive vacations, and cheating on our diets. We are back to road rage, being late for church, screaming at our neighbors, and taking our loved ones for granted.

September 11 seems so far away now that the lessons we vowed to never forget barely penetrate the surface anymore.

I have noticed changes over the years. There can now be heard a subtle variation of inflection in the voice of the people. Propaganda has taken over and I suspect that in the years to come there will be many differences in both story and theory. Society will probably create fantastic fairy tales, movies of intrigue, cover-ups, and grandiose conspiracies that fuel our imaginations and re-arouse our anger. The mystery surrounding that day will probably even inspire urban legends.

Politicians will most certainly continue their political games. Social summits and waving banners will rise higher and higher until people tire of it all, and one day the pleas to never forget will become the backdrop for backyard barbeques, greeting cards, and parades.

Still, as some of us rejoin society, others are yet glancing over their shoulders at our Middle Eastern citizens; still reeling from the terror and searching for ways to express the "so much" of emotion that guides or misguides them in their daily attempts at life, and back to business through the remains at ground zero.

For me, though I don't live in fear, and death has lost its sting, it seems like only yesterday that I died at the foot of those towers and my appointed journey began. I have paused from time to time to catch my breath, notice some new occurrence, or take note of the changing times.

Each time I have waited longer and longer to exhale, savoring the aroma of life and dancing in all its brilliance. Because for me, having lived an awakening, life is sweeter now and my every breath is engaged.

In my estimation, we should all breathe a little easier because we are all survivors. September 11 victimized all of us in one way or another, and each of us has a story to tell about it—when the terror began and where it ended. Every one of us can recall a smell or a song or what was on television in those very moments that the Twins fell.

> It seems like only yesterday that I died at the foot of those towers and my appointed journey began.

Every one of us can remember exactly what we were doing when we heard, "Terrorism will not stand."

It all began as just another Tuesday morning. We were going about our lives; working at our desks and reading e-mails, watching the morning news and talking on our phones, traveling and having our early morning coffee and cranberry muffins. We dressed in our familiar and went about the business of living.

Then somewhere alongside an airplane and a warped sense of justice, it evolved into something much bigger than just another Tuesday.

It became priorities, friendships, families, time lost, and time spent. It was about hope, penance, and giving. In my opinion, every detail and every single gut-wrenching incident in that day combined and became one very complex experience and simple definition. Sacrifice.

Sacrifice: To destroy, surrender, or suffer to be lost, for the sake of obtaining something; to give up in favor of a higher or more imperative object or duty; to devote, with loss or suffering.

While America gave up the comforts of home, I said good-bye to twenty-two friends—twenty-two more than my mental capacity could accept. I read their tributes and sat awkwardly in rooms full of the loved ones they left behind. I made light conversation and tried desperately not to look into their eyes, all the time knowing that the answers they wanted—needed—stemmed from questions too painful to ask. The sound of their breaking hearts was mind-numbing, and because of it there is a pain behind these eyes that you will never know. The truth is, sometimes nothing can stop a heart from breaking.

We were alone, and so we came together to share our grief and face our fears. We bonded as extended family wanting to make sense of our world torn open. Almost holding up our chests with pictures of our lost loves, we hoped until all hope was exhausted and then sacrificed our rights to know.

I remember watching the news and seeing people lining the streets like refugees—carrying their candles, asking for help, and unable to accept the grim fate that their loved ones met. For days the news replayed messages left on answering machines, and buildings all over New York City displayed walls of photos placed by families searching.

"NEVER FORGET" rang out loud and clear.

It was almost lyrical. The atmosphere was so solemn that it became inspiring, art. Poets penned rhythms with a decidedly ancestral touch of sorrow. Songwriters and vocalists stirred in their souls. Churches were packed, and writers wrote verses that were almost maddening in their intensity of thought.

> Twins that dance in the heavens,
> Floating on air like sky jewelry
> one by one and into the dark . . .
> they pass away . . .

Crowds of people gathered around that empty lot. Correction, hundreds gawked at an empty tomb.

Then someone stopped the music. Very quietly and very discreetly, it was back to business as usual . . . back to school, back to work, back to church, to the laundry, to the supermarket, and all the insecurities.

As for me, I struggled with my faith. I wondered about the compassion of a Father who did not step in. I questioned the validity of a heaven that seemed so unattainable. I doubted the value of a God I could not touch, until He touched me. He gave me peace but left this thorn: that I never shared the gospel with my friends. I never loved it enough.

You see, I didn't expect that one day I would be the one left standing in a crowd of hundreds taking their last breath. I didn't know that my words would be the last words that someone else would ever hear.

I never knew life could make such demands.

I didn't expect that searching eyes would search my soul looking for answers and wanting to know "why me."

I never understood the accountability that comes with truth.

I didn't expect that my mind would hold so vast a burden of secrets in order that others might be spared—kept from breaking down.

I never accepted the responsibility that comes with real love.

And so I have learned that my life does not belong to me. I understand now how words exhale life, and I will never again hold my breath for so long a time as this.

> I have learned that my life does not belong to me.

I have relearned to inhale and then to exhale, and as I breathe through Him, the Lord, that is, something wonderful happens—distance. Space comes between my emotions and me, and it yields an unexpected but welcome gift—faith. My world broadens until my vision lifts high above the "soils of despair" and I am soaring. Hallelujah!!

Then Agrippa said to Paul, "Do you think that in such a short time you can persuade me to be a Christian?" Paul replied, "Short time or long—I pray God that not only you but all who are listening to me today may become what I am, except for these chains." (Acts 26:28–29)

Through these pages, you have seen my birth. You have heard of my fears and my desires. You have heard my witness of our Father's great love, and I have opened my heart for you. I wonder now if knowing of my life has affected yours at all. I wonder if hearing of my pain has connected you to yours and brought you to the conclusion that grace finds you wherever you might be. In fact, I pray this for you.

I pray for those yet burdened, that our Father's breath completes His perfect work of restoration—for those still searching, that the peace of the Holy Spirit brings rest. My hope in all is that He, the Son, uses the sum of my experiences to inspire a place in your heart for His heart, that you might see God.

I realize, of course, that it is not easy to look into the face of God, to let Him out of the box and see Him in places other than Sunday morning sermons. I have lived that too. I know that it is much more comfortable to look around Him.

However, a unique opportunity exists here. This is one of those rare chances to gain clarity of purpose—to look past tragedy and loss and see God in it. The chance to acknowledge our anger and still forgive and see God in it—to surrender comprehension of these workings to the fullness of time and see God in it—to accept the pain and then receive the peace, and with confidence see God in it all.

Hallelujah to the Lamb.

> Oh, give thanks to the Lord, for He is good! For His mercy endures forever. Who can utter the mighty acts of the Lord? Who can declare all His praise? (Psalm 106:1–2 NKJV)

There is nothing wrong with being back to the business of living. In fact, I am sure the Lord would have us do so. I am equally convinced of His will for our freedom. I believe, finally, that His authentic voice speaks restoration into our souls and gently reminds us through the ash that fell like snow, the crackling radios, and the tears that dropped like rain, of the few things that we should never forget.

Never forget that September 11, 2001, was a day that we put compassion over power. We saw heroes up close and they touched us. We saw love transform pain into healing, hate into tolerance, anger into compassion, and fear into peace.

We learned the meaning of life and we appreciated its uniqueness and its frailty. Americans took a collective breath and people from all religious backgrounds looked to heaven in one accord.

Never forget that for a while the notion of a living GOD was not insulting, and people flocked to churches to look for Him. Millions prayed in schools, on the streets, out loud on buses, and in courtrooms, and no one was offended. We saw people united by the universal power of love, and we relearned the Lord's Prayer.

We retrieved our heritage from basements and attics and hung flags boldly in windows, yards, and on front porches across America.

We learned that day to fight and to never surrender to an enemy in any form. We learned to hope and to believe, and our faith in each other was improved.

Never forget that amazingly, after all had been said and done, after the buildings fell and all the dust settled, the only thing left standing was an old piece of Tower One, scarred and stained and twisted into the shape of an old rusted cross. . . .

That cross still stands.

> And God shall wipe away all tears from their eyes; and there shall be no more death, neither sorrow, nor crying, neither shall there be any more pain: for the former things are passed away. (Revelation 21:4 KJV)

CHAPTER 19

Suddenly

I Believe

But when ye shall hear of wars and commotions, be not terrified: for these things must first come to pass; but the end is not by and by.

—LUKE 21:9 KJV

The battle rages on. . . .

The subject of the last days and the rapture of the church has always been of great interest among Christians. Throughout the years, we have jumped at the opportunity to interpret prophecy, and people have repeatedly tried to "guide" us toward the exact date of Christ's return.

Even the most inflexible of atheists who have "seen and heard it all" are drawn by the parallel of today's headlines and biblical prophecy; headlines that appear to be ripped straight from the pages of Daniel and Revelation are everywhere.

What is even more astounding is the breathtaking rapidity with

which they occur. Reports of worldwide financial strain, food short-
ages and poverty, the exploitation of innocence, war, terrorism, disease, and devastating disasters crowd the news. There are predictions
of more earthquakes, tsunamis, global warming, and an incredible
rate of damage to our ozone.

Never before in the history of man have terrorists carried out
sinister attacks on American soil, in the Middle East, and in Euro-
pean countries . . . at the same time. Never before have the world's
security, faith, and economy been strained to their very founda-
tions—simultaneously. Never before in history have we experienced
record numbers of hurricanes in one season, forcing forecasters at
the National Hurricane Center to use Greek letters to name them.
The 2005 season set records in nearly every category.

Our world has lost its limits and we don't know how to respond
or what to believe.

And so we search for answers. We seek out every possible solu-
tion that might explain away the "signs" now shining above our
heads like any night in New York City's Times Square.

Our quest has resulted in more books about the last days, sparked
special-interest news reports, and inspired news magazine shows to
offer up "heaven" as their topic.

Religious leaders are compelled to give explanations that the
masses can accept, and the "end times" is a hot discussion topic. But
there is more behind these signs than just reading material.

> And when these things begin to come to pass, then look up,
> and lift up your heads; for your redemption draweth nigh. (Luke
> 21:28 KJV)

Begin to hear.

I believe there is a vastness of life beyond our immediate awareness that influences our everyday lives. I believe that in that realm, September 11 represents more than what we are willing to say. Because whether we acknowledge it or not, I believe that every Christian who saw the Twins fall knew in his soul that some great spiritual threshold had just been crossed and there was no going back.

We knew the end was near. We knew that the lines were drawn. I believe that we are witness to a unique time in the history of the world.

September 11 found many of us in complacency. As Christian believers, we were off the mark and simply existing from day to day. We were lukewarm in our faith, self-centered in our desires, carnal in nature, and caught up in a search for the latest and greatest addiction to make us feel alive.

As a church body, we compromised the Word of God for an affinity with the world and holiness for the modern tactics of reaching the unchurched. Our congregations were indistinguishable from those outside the church, and our families were without godly example.

The corporate "we" sacrificed godliness and the anointing, placed our own desires ahead of God's will, and closed our eyes to the certainty of a dying generation. I know I did.

Then alas, truth did prevail. In that vastly gruesome and powerful day, "Truth" yielded a cornerstone—a catalyst that compelled me, if not us, to lift our visions higher than the natural so that our hearts might see the glory of the Lord.

Baruch Hashem Adonai! Blessed be the Name of the Lord!

So even if we do not agree on the intrinsic worth of the spiritual lessons and encounters that I have written here, I believe the signs and implications of what happened on September 11, 2001, are much too powerful to ignore.

Now brace yourself.

> The signs and implications of what happened on September 11, 2001, are much too powerful to ignore.

For the Lord himself will come down from heaven, with a loud command, with the voice of the archangel and with the trumpet call of God, and the dead in Christ will rise first. (1 Thessalonians 4:16)

I believe the signs we are seeing today most certainly point to the rapture of the church. These are indeed end times. I believe that one day very soon, Jesus Christ himself will come in the clouds and millions of people will see their battles end. *Selah.*

After that, we who are still alive and are left will be caught up together with them in the clouds to meet the Lord in the air. . . . (1 Thessalonians 4:17)

Begin to understand.

I believe that followers of Christ from all around the world, of every race, creed, color, age, economic standing, and religious affiliation will vanish in a single moment of time . . . gone. The Word of God describes it as a "twinkling of an eye." In an instant, there will be boardrooms without directors, classrooms without teachers, hospitals without doctors and nurses, cars without drivers, airplanes without pilots, and loved ones disappearing mid-sentence and midmorning coffee. I am sure that complete chaos won't even begin to describe it. I imagine a worldwide crescendo of screaming voices.

When the dust clears, everyone left on earth will know emptiness beyond description and a greater sense of evil than has ever even been thought to exist. It will be the condition of things. Overwhelming sadness, confusion, loss, and insecurity will be worldwide.

It will happen at that time, even as it did on that September morning.

Begin to believe.

And so we will be with the Lord forever. (1 Thessalonians 4:17)

CHAPTER 20

Beside Still Waters

The Island

Today I look beyond the obvious and allow
miracles to be created in my life.
—AUTHOR UNKNOWN

My relationship with the Lord is the best part of me. It defines who I am. At this point in my life, I can't imagine life with any other. Most days I wake listening to my soul singing to Him.

We talk a lot, the Lord and I. I often sneak off by myself and create scenarios to do just that. Doing so keeps Him real for me. It keeps me from seeing Him as a distant God, peering out of the windows of heaven. He is my loving Father who meets me in my quiet place.

Imagine this.

Suddenly I am alone on an island. The island is tranquil, vast, and complete. There is beauty beyond my vision and my view extends out forever. The air is quiet here, and as I relax near the water's edge and into the soothing warmth of the sun, I haven't a care in the world.

I read somewhere once that beauty is a revelation. If that is true, in this place, I am made wise beyond my years.

The sand is wet and thick where the occasional waves rise and break on the shore. Splashing over my legs and feet, they flow deep and warm. I am nearly enraptured when every now and then an almost invisible mist settles on my face. This is paradise. And everything is perfect when I can nearly taste the smell of salt in the air now settling on my lips.

Not that it needed more, mind you, but when I lit a candle to add more ambience, there He was . . . Jesus, the Christ.

My first impression was that He is much different from what I imagined all those years. I guess I was looking for the man in the picture over Momma's bed—the man with one hand in the air and a lamb on His lap. Instead, I saw someone strong, confident . . . more than simply ordinary.

As He approached, the shadows from the tress that lined the shore provided a striking silhouette behind Him. My question: Will my heart ever beat in normal rhythm again?

At first greeting, I was intimidated. After all, this was HIM—the Holy One, the Lamb of God, the great I AM. I wanted to be impressive. I wanted to present myself to Him whole and acceptable. That never happened.

Instead, I smiled that awkward smile, and when I leaned in to meet His effort to hug me, I gave Him one of those weak, insecure hugs . . . patting His back as if I were burping a baby.

He laughed aloud and said, "You've pulled away from people since you were a child, especially strangers. But I'm no stranger, little one." He grabbed me and greeted me as if we were long-lost friends. It was amazing. My heart nearly leaped from my chest. I was so nervous and so in awe . . . that I settled down only when Jesus sat with me on the shore and started talking.

He told me about my first steps. I told Him about my first date. He explained to me my first fears. I cried about my first heartbreak. Then both of us laughed about the time I did that hugely embarrassing thing in high school. We laughed together. Never once did He accuse me or make me feel bad about being me.

Never did He point His finger or bring to light the fact that I have always been somewhat eccentric . . . a cracked pot. In fact, it was completely the opposite. I felt useful. Somehow, looking back with Him, all those little things in life that made me cry were just that . . . little things.

Across the ocean the sky was a deep blue as the sun began to set. Few clouds were in the sky, but those that hung on the horizon created the most beautiful shades of reds, oranges, and purples. When it struck me that He is the artist behind this awesome canvas, I felt unworthy to be in His company. I am sure He recognized my being ill at ease when I made that goofy laughing sound that I make when I am nervous. He responded lightheartedly, patting my shoulder like a pal would do. "It's okay. It's all right," He said. The sound of His voice, together with the sounds of the ocean, was almost hypnotic. The calm of His presence gave me comfort.

"Do you remember the time you were so depressed that you could barely hear my voice?" He asked. "I prompted a little boy in the pizza shop to make silly noises at you while he ate ice cream. You thought it was so funny that you laughed out loud . . . in public.

"Remember how awkward you were coming into adulthood, how badly you hurt because you didn't fit in with the in crowd. I wanted so much to hold you then. But I knew that if I didn't let you live it, you'd never know it."

The light from the candle flickered when I exhaled. Suddenly there was clarity. If the Lord didn't let me live it, I would never know it . . .

Faith. . . .

We sat quietly for a little while as I tried to absorb all that He had shared. He smiled at me again and gently rubbed His hand over mine. It was such a sweet moment, and He was so beautiful.

Then in a scene that resembled one I had read before, Jesus knelt in the sand and began making circles with His fingertip. Without looking up at me, He asked, "Do you love me?" Before I could open my mouth, He continued, "You're all I've ever loved." I responded in my usual tongue-tied state. I blabbered out something preposterous like, "What? You mean me?"

A seagull flew overhead.

He went on. "What if I had never come?" I turned to look at Him. "What if my grace was not and life was left to the goodness of humanity?" I looked away in embarrassment. "Would you call for me or curse me?" I tried to speak. "And what of your soul?" I fought to understand. "What if you were right now in your eternity and time was no more?" The water washed up over the shore and I felt its warmth move between my toes. He rose and turned to me. "Where would you yet live?" He asked. There were tears in His eyes.

Just then, in that instant, I saw His eyes. I recognized them. They were the eyes of that trembling father in a smoke-filled room on the ninety-third floor of Tower One, dialing his little girls for the last time. Those were the eyes behind that calming voice singing "Amazing Grace" in a crowded and slippery stairwell, trapped out-more split apart one evil from the other. It has no varying degrees. Death is death.

> For the wages of sin is death; but the gift of God is eternal life through Jesus Christ our Lord. (Romans 6:23 NKJV)

One morning a month or so after the attack, I woke up with an achy body, red swollen eyes, and personally one of the most upsetting stories that I had heard about the terrorist attacks to date.

A friend told me he had read an article that reported that after seeing the fall of the Twin Towers on television, thousands of Palestinians paraded through cities in the West Bank and Gaza, celebrating. My friend heard that U.S. news executives decided not to broadcast the footage because they feared Americans would retaliate against citizens from the Middle East.

I was sick. Was that it? Was all that horror simply a matter of "I win, you lose"?

> ## Was all that horror simply a matter of "I win, you lose"?

I was furious. I felt victimized all over again, and I couldn't understand how one human being could find pleasure in the sufferings of another.

Then once again, but not suddenly, God's grace was sufficient. It provided enough distance between me, that particular day, and the events of September 11, so that I could begin to see enough through the fog to discern some insight regarding the sinful, combative nature of man.

> The heart is deceitful above all things, and desperately wicked: Who can know it? (Jeremiah 17:9 NKJV)

side a roof door when the ceilings began to cave. The eyes of the people who stayed behind with the handicapped victims waiting for police officers who never made it up the stairs. Those were the eyes of firemen who pushed me to safety, the doctor who cared for me for more than a year free of charge, the therapist who visited my home regularly so that I could sleep a little, the children who loved me, the brother who prayed nonstop, and the pastor who became my friend. Those were the eyes of God.

Before I could say with my mouth what my soul was screaming, tears poured down my face like a waterfall. "It was you . . . every time . . . you?" Repentance washed over me. "I'm so sorry," I whispered. I grabbed Him as tightly as I could. "Please, Jesus," I cried, "forgive me for looking past you time after time. Forgive me for seeing you only in the obvious places. I never even thought to look outside the box."

He moved closer to me, put His hand underneath my chin, slowly lifted my bowed head, and kissed me very gently on my nose. "You're all I've ever loved," He said.

I placed my head on His chest and drifted off to the sounds of His beating heart. I responded in a whisper. "You're all I've ever longed for."

Most of us have found ourselves on that island with the Lord—in that critical juncture where the uncertainty of life, death, and all the questions of our purpose meet us head-on. In such a place, these things are never more beside the point and yet never more critical!

We have reached that juncture, my friend.

If you already know Jesus Christ, then you should already be in love. If not, let me suggest that you get reacquainted with an old friend. Look again at His personality, His sense of humor, His smile,

His role in your life, His desire to be your closest Love, and . . . His eyes. There's nothing wrong with rekindling an old flame.

If you don't know Jesus Christ, I sincerely hope that somehow, some word or prayer that I have shared has awakened your curiosity or your thirst for Him. I hope that you invite Him into your life as Savior and Lord. In fact, please do. Find time to get to know Him and fall in love. Believe me, there is none greater. His are the eyes you have been looking for.

Wherever you find yourself, saved or unsaved, I invite you to come and see a man. . . .

For this is what the Lord says: "I will extend peace to her like a river, and the wealth of nations like a flooding stream." (Isaiah 66:12)

Final Words

I speak without reservation of what I know and who I am. In doing so, I am aware that all people have the right to truth. In truth, no matter how uncompromising, there are certain liberties that birth salvation.

So as you close this book and your mind begins the process of rightly dividing the Word of truth, which I encourage you to do, know that I am living proof that God's grace really is sufficient for our needs.

It is in obedience to Him that I deliver a final message to you, His friend.

If you forget most of what I have said: that life is fragile and fleeting, that we are temporary here on earth and no "thing" matters, that God's plan is too immense for human knowledge, and we should surrender comprehension of it to the fullness of time. . . . If by some chance it slips your mind that we should pledge to one another our love as a commitment and not a sentiment, at least hold on to the sum of it all.

The sum being that life is a wonderful love story filled to overflowing with joy and sadness and peace and upset and love and hope and tragedy, disappointment, children, birthdays, holidays, sports, great tools, speaking in tongues, music, poetry, chocolate ice cream, lollipops, and the eyes of God.

The clearer view is the importance of not how we die but how we live. That we grow beyond ourselves and learn to forgive, that we find peace in surrendering our lives to do good works, that we regularly touch somebody's life and walk profoundly steadfast in our faith in God and His purpose. Having done all, we will stand unwavering through life's falling towers, whatever they might be, until one glorious day, after having suffered the "slings and arrows of outrageous fortune," your journey will deliver you into the arms of God, and God himself will welcome you into His bosom and crown you with His own hand.

Imagine . . . the eternal breath of life.

My final words are a prayer.

THANK YOU, HOLY FATHER, for allowing me to speak freely to you about everything. Thank you for setting me up with great expectations—that I can ask anything for the sake of your kingdom and know I will hear from you. According to that promise, I ask today that my words will be inspired and that you would use them to draw your children to yourself. Bless your children, that they might experience the joys and fulfillment of intimacy in a relationship with you. Help all of us to see you more clearly and realize that we have nothing without you. Help us, Father, to love you better.

*N*ow unto Him who is able to keep us from falling, and to present us faultless before the presence of His glory with exceeding joy, to the only wise God our Savior, be glory and majesty, dominion and power, both now and forever.

Amen.

About the Author

LESLIE HASKIN is one of fifteen children born of humble beginnings to a Baptist minister in Chicago. Her drive for success and independence led her to New York in 1987, and later to Kemper Insurance Company in 2001, where she achieved great success. She became the director of operations and one of only two African-Americans to hold executive title within the corporation's eastern region. Her office was on the thirty-sixth floor of the World Trade Center, Tower One, where on September 11, 2001, she almost lost her life.

Today this single parent is active in outreach ministry. In addition to her career, Leslie serves with Goodwill Evangelical Presbyterian Church in Montgomery, New York. She spends her time in the inner city spreading the message of hope to the homeless and otherwise lost. She is the founder of a ministry designed to provide rehabilitation and healing to women and children who are homeless and victims of domestic violence. She also organizes conferences and other events for singles in the Hudson River valley.

Leslie has appeared at several memorials honoring the victims and survivors of 9/11. She has served as keynote speaker at national and regional conferences throughout the United States, including The West Point Women of the Chapel, North American Missions Board—World Changes, and The Place of Surrender Singles Conference. She lives in upstate New York.

Timeline

September 11, 2001

8:46 A.M.
Terrorists crash American Airlines Flight 11 into the World Trade Center's north tower, floors 93–99.

9:03 A.M.
Terrorists crash United Airlines Flight 175 into the south tower, floors 77–85.

9:37 A.M.
Terrorists crash American Airlines Flight 77 into the Pentagon.

9:59 A.M.
The south tower collapses.

10:03 A.M.
Hijacked United Airlines Flight 93 crashes near Shanksville, Pennsylvania.

10:28 A.M.
The north tower collapses.

The attacks on the World Trade Center killed 2,749 people. In all, 2,973 people died as a result of the attacks on September 11, 2001.

World Trade Center Complex

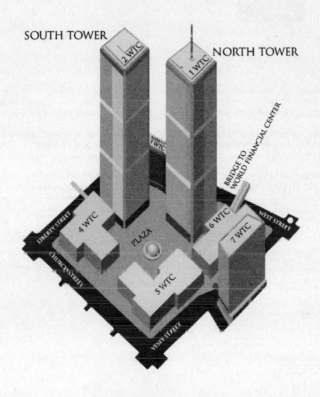

SOUTH TOWER

2 WTC

NORTH TOWER

1 WTC

1 WTC

BRIDGE TO
WORLD FINANCIAL CENTER

4 WTC

6 WTC

7 WTC

WEST STREET

PLAZA

5 WTC

LIBERTY STREET

CHURCH STREET

VESEY STREET

Kemper
Insurance Companies

April 18, 2002

Leslie Haskins

███████████████████████

Re: Long Term Disability   **Certified Mail**

███████████████████

Dear Ms. Haskins:

We have reviewed your claim for continuing eligibility for Kemper's disability leave policy. Based on the information available to us, you are no longer eligible for Kemper disability leave.

In the Illness/disability leave of absence policy, it states that if your absence is six or more working days, physician certification of your illness, injury or other covered medical condition is required. Certification may also be required for attendance and family medical leave purposes.

When certification is required for illness/disability leave purposes, the certification process and definition of disability is the same as in the salary continuation and long term disability plans. This means your absence must be certified in accordance with those plans.

Our records reflect your disability commenced on October 31, 2001. Therefore, you must be unable to perform the material and substantial duties of your occupation as a Branch Services Director.

Information received from Ariella ████████ LCSW, indicates that you are released to return to work with the following restrictions: no crossing bridges, entering tunnels, or traveling to New York City. Per review of your job requirement form, the above restrictions are not material and substantial duties of your occupation as a Branch Services Director; therefore, you are no longer eligible for Kemper's disability leave.

We have notified your Human Resources Department of this determination.

If you have any questions or additional information that may affect our decision, please feel free to contact me in this office as soon as possible.

KEMPER EMPLOYEE 501 (C)
(9) BENEFIT TRUST
Employee Claim Department, K-1

(847) 320-4079
One Kemper Drive, Long Grove, IL, 60049-0001

www.kemperinsurance.com

Determining my employment status and subsequent settlement was a long process. Sometimes the points that were made seemed silly, like these shown in the highlighted paragraph. (It was impossible for me to get to work without crossing bridges and going through tunnels, and, of course, my office was in the city.) In fairness to Kemper, this was an unprecedented event; no one knew how to decide such a case. In the end, everything worked out well.

American Red Cross

Date: 5/30/03

September 11 Recovery Program
150 Amsterdam Avenue
New York, NY 10023
(877) 746-4987

Dear Provider: ~~&~~ Dr. William Rohan,

The American Red Cross is currently reviewing a request for financial assistance from your patient, Mr.(Ms.)Mrs. _Leslie Hastin_ . In order to process this request we need limited information from your office. We have enclosed a copy of a release of information from him/her for your files. Please print your answers to these brief questions below, sign the letter, and send it to us using the enclosed pre-addressed envelope.

1. Did your patient sustain an injury or medical condition on 9/11/01 that was a direct result of the events of that day? Please circle (Yes) or No

2. What was the injury or condition that occurred as a direct result of 9/11/01? (1) Post Traumatic Stress Disorder
(2) Multiple Contusions

3. When did this patient first seek medical treatment for this injury or medical condition? Please give the full date (day/month/year) _9·12·01_

4. What date did the patient seek medical care in your office (day/month/year) _9·12·01_ ?

5. Is this injury or condition expected to need on-going medical treatment? Please circle: (Yes) or No

6. If the patient needs on-going treatment, please indicate how much longer the treatment is expected to continue _Unknown is under the care of a Psychotherapist_

7. If the patient no longer needs treatment, please give the date of the last treatment. Please give the full date (day/month/year)_____

Important Note: DO NOT SEND MEDICAL RECORDS.

Provider's Name: _William Rohan_ License # ████████████
Provider's Signature: ████████████   Date: _6/10/03_

Thank you for your cooperation in this matter. If you have any questions about this form, please call me 212-███

Sincerely,

████████████

████████████

Assistant Director, Health Services
American Red Cross, September 11 Recovery Program

████████████████████████████████████

Rev. 11/25/02

The September 11 Recovery Program was amazing. It helped many people financially, emotionally, and mentally. For me, it was a lifeline. All those dollars that were contributed really did do a lot of good!

GEORGE E. PATAKI
GOVERNOR

JOAN A. CUSACK
CHAIRWOMAN

STATE OF NEW YORK
EXECUTIVE DEPARTMENT
CRIME VICTIMS BOARD

BOARD MEMBERS
CHRISTINA HERNANDEZ
CHARLES F. MAROTTA
JACQUELINE C. MATTINA
BENEDICT J. MONACHINO

June 6, 2003

Re: Television Broadcast of the Criminal Trial of Zacarias Moussaoui for the
September 11, 2001 World Trade Center, Pentagon and Pennsylvania attacks.

Dear Claimant:

I am writing to you to inform you of the opportunity to view the Closed Circuit
Television (CCTV) Broadcast of the Criminal Trial of Zacarias Moussaoui. This trial
may be viewed from rooms in federal courthouses in the District of Columbia,
Manhattan, Long Island and Newark, New Jersey.

A person is eligible to view the CCTV broadcast if (1) he/she suffered direct
physical harm from the events of September 11, 2001 and was present at the scene
of the terrorist acts when they occurred or immediately thereafter; or (2) he/she is the
spouse, legal guardian, parent, child, brother or sister of a victim who died, is
severely injured, is incapacitated, is under 18 years of age, or has a disability that
requires assistance of another person for mobility.

If you are interested in viewing the Moussaoui trial I have enclosed an
Application to View the CCTV Broadcast which you must complete and return to the
following address **before June 20, 2003**:

The United States Attorney's Office
Eastern District of Virginia
2100 Jamieson Avenue
Alexandria, Virginia 22314
Attention: Victim Witness Unit

The US Attorney's Office will let you know directly if your application is accepted. It is
hoped that the trial of this case will begin this Fall.

Yours truly,

Joan A. Cusack
Chairwoman

845 CENTRAL AVENUE. Room 107
ALBANY. NEW YORK 12206-1588
(518) 457-8727

55 HANSON PLACE. Room 1000
BROOKLYN. NEW YORK 11217-1523
(718) 923-4325

65 COURT STREET. Room 308
BUFFALO. NEW YORK 14202-3406
(716) 847-7992

I was invited to watch the trial of Zacarias Moussaoui on closed circuit TV in 2006. It was much too
painful to view in its entirety. But after the trial, I was invited to make a statement to the media: "As
a WTC survivor who narrowly escaped the burning towers, I found the trial of Zacarias Moussaoui
intensely personal and extremely painful to watch. As a nation, we've suffered through hearing tapes
of our loved ones fighting for their lives; old wounds have reopened, and once again, we find ourselves
asking why. No doubt, some understanding will help us to heal, but God alone will give us strength
to forgive. Only God has given me the strength to forgive Zacarias Moussaoui. I don't love him and
I'm not ready to embrace him, but I have forgiven him. I pray this peace for the nation. Leslie Haskin."